Creating an Effective Mystagogy

A Handbook for Catechetical Leaders

ST. MARY'S CHURCH CRESCENT
86 CHURCH HILL RD.
CRESCENT, NY 12188-1126

Dennis Chriszt, CPPS

Resource Publications, Inc.
San Jose, California

Reprint Department
Resource Publications, Inc.
160 E. Virginia Street #290
San Jose, CA 95112-5876
(408) 286-8505 (voice)
(408) 287-8748 (fax)

Library of Congress Cataloging-in-Publication Data
Chriszt, Dennis, 1954–
    Creating an effective mystagogy : a handbook for catechetical teams / Dennis Chriszt.
        p.   cm.
    Includes bibliographical references.
    ISBN 0-89390-515-1
        1. Mystagogy—Catholic Church. 2. Catechetics—Catholic Church. 3. Initiation rites—Religious aspects—Catholic Church. I. Title.
    BX1968 .C48 2001
    268'.82—dc21

                                                                2001019612

Printed in the United States of America.
01 02 03 04 05 | 5 4 3 2 1

Editorial director: Nick Wagner
Production: Romina Saha
Copyeditor: Laura Quilling
Cover design: Mike Sagara

To the memory of
three mystagogues:
Ralph Kiefer,
Christiane Brusselmans,
and
Jim Dunning

Contents

Preface ix

Abbreviations xi

Introduction: Focusing on Mystagogy 1

My Experience with Mystagogy 1

The Experience of Mystagogy in the Church
in the United States of America 6

Critical Reflection on the Present Situation 8

The Christian Story and Vision 11

Some Challenges Presented by the Rite
and by Present Practices 15

In Search of an Effective Mystagogy? 17

A Mystagogical Method 21

Chapter 1: Present Mystagogical Practices
in Three Parishes 27

St. Ambrose of Milan Parish:
Archdiocese of St. Paul and Minneapolis 27

St. Cyril of Jerusalem Parish:
Archdiocese of St. Paul and Minneapolis 33

St. John Chrysostom Parish:
Archdiocese of Cincinnati 42

Chapter 2: Analysis of the Present Practices. . . . 57

An Effective Mystagogy 58

Inquirers Come with Several Strong Desires. 59

Many People Play Significant Roles
in the Initiation Process 61

The Process Is Focused on a Life of Faith 65

Some Conclusions 70

Chapter 3: The Church's Vision of Mystagogy . . . 75

The Ancient Tradition 75

A Contemporary Vision 93

Chapter 4: A Conversation with Present Practices and the Church's Vision of Mystagogy 109

In Search of ... ? 110

What Are the Goals of an Initiation Process
That Is Mystagogical Throughout? 112

What Is the Context in Which an Authentically
Mystagogical Initiation Process Occurs? 120

Who Are the Significant People in an Authentically
Mystagogical Initiation Process? 128

How Does the Tradition Affirm and Challenge
Present Initiatory Practices? 134

Chapter 5: Suggestions for a Contemporary Mystagogical Practice 139

Starting at the End: Be Clear about the Goals 140

Back to the Beginning: Mystagogical Throughout 143

Ministers of Initiation: Mystagogues All 157

The Search Continues 162

Appendix 1: Excerpts from RCIA 1974 165

Appendix 2: Excerpts from RCIA 1988 169

Notes 175

Bibliography 203

Preface

When I started the search for an effective mystagogy, I thought I already knew where it would lead. I imagined a final chapter with an outline of a process that one could use for catechetical sessions during the period of postbaptismal catechesis or mystagogy. I thought that mystagogy *was* the period of postbaptismal catechesis. I believed that by interviewing a number of neophytes and their mystagogues, I would confirm what I already believed from my own experience as a mystagogue. I was wrong. The search took me in directions I never would have imagined.

I had also believed that I could learn little from a group of fourth-century bishops whose world was very different from the world we live in today. Again, I was wrong. The more I read of the preaching of Cyril of Jerusalem, Ambrose of Milan, John Chrysostom, and Theodore of Mopsuestia, the more turns I took on my search for an effective mystagogy. In the beginning I never imagined that I would actually have wanted to read all the mystagogical homilies of these men, let alone their catechetical preaching. They led me to places in my own spiritual life I am grateful to have gone. I was surprised on several occasions when I chose to quote these great preachers in my own preaching during Lent and Eastertime.

I was surprised also by the conclusions at which I arrived. In the beginning I never would have guessed how significant the role of the preacher would become. Nor would I have thought that the *Constitution on the Sacred Liturgy*'s statement on the real presence of Christ in the assembly gathered, in the word proclaimed, in the rituals celebrated, and in the ministers ministering would become such a significant foundation for developing an effective mystagogy and an authentic initiation experience. I never would have suspected that the distinction between postbaptismal catechesis and mystagogy would also have become so significant to the search for an effective mystagogy.

I hope you will read every chapter and not jump too quickly to the suggestions for a contemporary mystagogy in the last chapter. This entire book is meant to be an experience of mystagogy—a journey from experience to new insights and challenges for future living. If you look only to the conclusions, you will have missed the trip, and in the process, you will have missed many of the insights gained only by one who has taken the trip.

I am, of course, immensely grateful to the catechists and neophytes of the five parishes I had the opportunity to visit as part of this book. Their willingness to share their stories of faith with a stranger who was going to analyze what they said for a doctoral book was a great gift to me. As you read some of their comments, know that the whole story is much richer than the small excerpts contained herein.

I am also grateful to the many colleagues who asked the right questions and pointed me in the right directions when I would have gone astray by myself. I am especially grateful to Ed Foley, O.F.M.Cap., who guided me through the process of writing and rewriting. I am also thankful to my fellow Missionaries of the Precious Blood for their support and encouragement and for the many opportunities they provided me over the years that helped me be where I am today. I owe a debt of gratitude to many others, many who don't even know how they helped me along the way. I ask God's blessings on them all.

Dennis Chriszt, CPPS

Abbreviations

AT	*Apostolic Tradition* — Hippolytus
BH	*Baptismal Homilies* — Theodore of Mopsuestia
BI	*Baptismal Instructions* — John Chrysostom
CCC	*Catechism of the Catholic Church*
CCL	*Code of Canon Law*
CSL	*Constitution on the Sacred Liturgy* — Vatican II
DCMA	*Decree on the Church's Missionary Activity* — Vatican II
ET	*Egeria's Travels* — Egeria
FIYH	*Fulfilled in Your Hearing: The Homily in the Sunday Assembly* — National Conference of Catholic Bishops
GI	*Christian Initiation: General Introduction* (to the *Rite of Christian Initiation of Adults*)
GIRM	*General Instruction of the Roman Missal*
GNLYC	*General Norms for the Liturgical Year and the Calendar*
ICEL	International Commission on English in the Liturgy
MC	*Mystagogic Catecheses* — Cyril of Jerusalem
NSC	*National Statutes for the Catechumenate* — National Conference of Catholic Bishops
OS	*On the Sacraments* — Ambrose of Milan
RCIA	*Rite of Christian Initiation of Adults — Complete text of the rite together with additional rites approved for use in the dioceses of the United States of America (1988)*
RCIA 1974	*Rite of Christian Initiation of Adults — Provisional text approved for interim use in the dioceses of the United States of America by the Bishops' Committee on Liturgy and the Executive Committee of the National Conference of Catholic Bishops and confirmed by the Apostolic See (1974)*

Introduction

Focusing on Mystagogy

> Liturgical catechesis aims to initiate people into the mystery of Christ (It is "mystagogy.") by proceeding from the visible to the invisible, from the sign to the thing signified, from the "sacraments" to the "mysteries" (CCC 1075).[1]

When I began to write this book, my goal was to help parishes design processes that enable people, especially neophytes, to experience the mystery of Christ and to reflect on and to live out of that experience throughout their lives. More specifically, it was to examine what was happening in mystagogy,[2] so that the gift to the church that is mystagogy might be used more effectively for the sake of the reign of God.

My experience of mystagogy, the experience of the fourth-century mystagogues, and the experience of mystagogues and neophytes in the United States today will be the starting point for this exploration.

My Experience with Mystagogy

I first encountered mystagogy while attending the Beginnings and Beyond Institute sponsored by the North American Forum on the Catechumenate.[3] Until then, mystagogia, as it was called in 1984, was a complete mystery to me. While I had been a catechist and parish director of Christian initiation of adults for several years, I had no idea what to do during the period of postbaptismal catechesis. I had read the introductions in the *Rite of the Christian Initiation of Adults*,[4] but I had no experience or understanding of what it was all about.

One of the presenters at that institute, Ron Oakham, introduced the participants to what he called *ritual catechesis*,[5] a method for reflecting on a ritual experience. Together we both practiced and discussed that method. We also considered its implications for mystagogia. My experience of ritual catechesis and the subsequent discussions among those of us on the Beyond track during that institute had a profound influence on my future ministry as a mystagogue. That catechetical method became the method I used both in celebrating mystagogy in the two parishes where I subsequently ministered as a mystagogue and in teaching adults about sacraments in other catechetical situations.

During the following Easter season, several other mystagogues and I used the ritual catechesis method we had learned the previous summer in a small town just outside a major metropolitan area. There were about twelve hundred families, 90 percent of whom were first- or second-generation Americans of Eastern European descent. The town itself was over 90 percent Catholic with six Catholic parishes for some four thousand people. The town was dominated by three companies, all of which had moved their corporate headquarters into the nearby city during the previous two decades. It was a rather stable community. Although many children moved away as adults, few new families moved into the community. With so few people in the town who were not already baptized Roman Catholics, it was considered rare that anyone would seek initiation into the Catholic Church as an adult. But in the late summer of 1983, my second year as an associate pastor, each of the three full-time priests on the staff had encountered two or three persons who expressed an interest in becoming Catholic, and so we formed an initiation team and used the ritual and catechetical processes described in the *Rite of Christian Initiation of Adults*.

The following year, two members of the initiation team attended the Beginnings and Beyond Institute. During the Easter season of 1985, I experienced mystagogy for the first time.

Susan had been baptized just two days earlier, and she was crying.[6] The neophytes, their sponsors and spouses, and the members of the parish initiation team had gathered to remember, to reflect, and to rejoice. We had gathered around the waters of the font, the waters in which Susan and three others had been baptized. We had listened again to the Easter story of resurrection. We had blessed ourselves (some of us, like Susan, for the first time) with the water blessed two nights earlier by the light of the Easter candle. We had prayed for one another and joined our prayers together with the prayer that Jesus taught us. When we had gathered in the living room of the parish pastoral center, Susan began crying.

As mystagogue for that evening gathering of postbaptismal catechesis, I invited those who were gathered together to remember not only what we had just celebrated, but also what we had experienced a couple of days earlier at the Easter Vigil. Then I invited those who wanted to share their experience to do so.

Susan then told us this story:

I had a hard time sleeping last Friday night. It had been a long day. But in the morning, Holy Saturday morning, I woke up filled with all kinds of strange feelings. For some reason, I knew that what had happened to Jesus was about to happen to me. By the time the day was over, I would be dead. I was not sick, but I was certainly dying.

There were so many people to talk to. If this was to be the last day of my life, there were so many people to talk to. I talked to my children. I told them I loved them. I asked them if they could forgive me for the times I had let them down, for the times I had been less of a mother than I could have—should have—been.

I called my ex-husbands—all three of them. I doubt if they understood what I was doing. But I made peace with each of them in my own way. I asked for their forgiveness for the many ways in which I had hurt them during our marriages, and I offered them my forgiveness. I needed to be reconciled with each of them before I died.

I called my parents, my brothers and sisters, even my ex-in-laws. I thanked them all for the ways in which they had supported and loved me over the years. They must have thought I was crazy, calling them for no apparent reason and offering them my love and asking for their forgiveness.

But I was dying, and I knew I'd be dead before the day was over.

And then we gathered in church to pray and to prepare ourselves for the Easter Vigil; it was like making my own funeral arrangements. You were all so excited about what was about to happen, and so was I. But I knew that I was about to die and that

made my excitement and anxiety just a little different.
And then, during the Easter Vigil, when you poured that water
over my head, then I died ... I died.

When she finished her story, many in the group were in tears.
After a brief period of silence, I shared the following Scripture passage
with the neophytes and their sponsors:

Are you unaware that we who were baptized into Christ Jesus were
baptized into his death? We were indeed buried with him through
baptism into death, so that, just as Christ was raised from the dead
by the glory of the Father, we too might live in newness of life.
   For if we have grown into union with him through a death like
his, we shall also be united with him in the resurrection. We know
that our old self was crucified with him, so that our sinful body
might be done away with, that we might no longer be in slavery to
sin. For a dead person has been absolved from sin. If, then, we have
died with Christ, we believe that we shall also live with him. We
know that Christ, raised from the dead, dies no more; death no
longer has power over him. As to his death, he died to sin once and
for all; as to his life, he lives for God. Consequently, you too must
think of yourselves as [being] dead to sin and living for God in
Christ Jesus (Rom 6:3–11).

This was the same Scripture passage we had heard at the Easter
Vigil, the epistle for that evening. But in this context, on this night, it
came to life in a new way. Connections were made. The tradition was
shared. The starting point for these connections and sharing was
Susan's experience.
   This reading also reminded Eleanor, another neophyte, of another
recent experience. A few weeks earlier, George, one of the candidates
for full communion, had a massive heart attack. All the catechumens,
candidates, sponsors, and catechists from our community had visited
him in the hospital and prayed with him sometime during the
following week. Some had witnessed his profession of faith,
confirmation, and first communion. Some were present as he was
anointed with the oil of the sick. By the end of that week, George died.

4

All gathered at the wake and again at his funeral the day after they had celebrated the third scrutiny.[7]

Remembering that event, Eleanor, the other neophytes, and those who gathered with them began to make connections between the symbols of water poured over those who were baptized just a few days earlier and the water splashed on George's casket just a few weeks earlier; the paschal candle that stood before those reborn to eternal life at the Easter Vigil and a similar candle that stood as a silent sentinel at George's funeral;[8] the white garments that wrapped the newly baptized and the white cloth laid on the casket of our friend. All these symbols spoke of the relationship between life and death, a relationship celebrated in baptism and in the *Order of Christian Funerals*. The words from Paul's Letter to the Romans, quoted above, which had been proclaimed at George's funeral, were also proclaimed at Susan's and Eleanor's baptism, just as the story of the resurrection of Lazarus was heard at both the third scrutiny and George's funeral. We remembered. We made connections. We experienced once again the presence of God in our midst. There were new understandings and new insights into the faith into which the neophytes had just recently been baptized, understandings and insights that would have been impossible prior to the experience.

That experience of mystagogy convinced me of its importance. It had an effect, not only on my way of thinking about mystagogy but also on my behaviors as a mystagogue, preacher, and presider at the rites of the Roman Catholic Church. It likewise was effective in that the neophytes who were part of the experience began to see the connections between their lives, liturgy, and the Christian tradition. This was my first real experience of mystagogy during the Christian initiation of adults,[9] and it is out of that experience that I come to this study.

I have experienced mystagogy many times since then. I have been both mystagogue and member of the Christian faithful. I have witnessed, rejoiced, and made connections in my own life as part of the mystagogical process. I have been blessed, and it is the blessings that I have received and the blessings I have shared with neophytes and other members of the Christian faithful that have convinced me of the importance of mystagogy and postbaptismal catechesis.

Like the Rite's authors, I have come to believe that "the period of postbaptismal catechesis is of *great significance* for both the neophytes and the rest of the faithful (RCIA 246).[10] I gained new understandings, new insights, and a deeper faith in God. The paschal mystery was opened up for me in new ways. The call to witness to the death and resurrection of Jesus the Christ was reinforced and reenergized.

The Experience of Mystagogy in the Church in the United States of America

In 1988 Liturgy Training Publications conducted a survey of catechists and parish directors of the Christian initiation of adults. While those who answered the survey were not statistically representational of the Catholic population in the United States, they do seem to form a kind of cross section of the American church. The most common responses to two different questions[11] indicated that of the RCIA stages or rites mystagogy seems most difficult to understand and most difficult to do (O'Brien 9). In the workshops that I have conducted in three different dioceses over the past twelve years, the participants seemed to support the survey results. Time and time again, I was asked to share resources and information that might enable catechists and parish directors of Christian initiation to both understand the goals of mystagogy and to help them plan for the postbaptismal catechesis that takes place during this stage of the initiation process.

James Dunning summed up the situation in this way:

We have no hard data, but we do have anecdotal evidence that some neophytes not only become passive but totally inactive regarding Sunday worship. Some suggest that this is not so much a matter of deliberate choice but of drifting away from active participation because the church has drifted away from them. The church that they experienced during initiation—a church of small groups round the Scriptures sharing faith—in effect no longer exists for them ("Demystifying Mystagogy" 32).

When I suggested to Dunning that perhaps as many as 50 percent of those initiated at the Easter Vigil cease to participate in the liturgical life of the church within two years of their initiation, he responded by calling me "an optimist." He indicated that from the feedback he received while conducting institutes and giving presentations at various conferences, many people he talked to thought the number would be larger and take place sooner. This may be an indication that something is awry. While many neophytes consider their experience of the Christian initiation of adults to be positive, its effects may not be long lasting, or at the very least, some of the expected behavioral results (for example, regular, active participation in the liturgical life of the parish community) are not in evidence.

Though anecdotal evidence seems to indicate that more and more parish initiation teams are doing something they call postbaptismal catechesis or mystagogy, the vast majority of parishes in the United States do not appear to be doing anything during or beyond the Easter season that they would call mystagogy. Some of this may indicate a misunderstanding of the term itself. The Rite indicates that the "main setting [for mystagogy] is the so-called Masses for neophytes, that is, the Sunday Masses of the Easter season" (RCIA 247). Most ministers of initiation, including the United States bishops, seem to believe that additional gatherings ought to be part of the Easter season and "should extend until the anniversary of Christian initiation, with at least monthly assemblies of the neophytes for their deeper Christian formation and incorporation into the full life of the Christian community" (*National Statutes for the Catechumenate* 24). What these *assemblies* look like remains unclear. To many ministers of initiation, the Rite seems to imply that some kind of catechetical gatherings ought to take place when it also calls mystagogy "the period of postbaptismal catechesis."

In the last few years, several published resources have been made available to assist parishes in doing postbaptismal catechesis.[12] The very existence of these resources seems to indicate that many people believe that mystagogy ought to include more than the Sunday eucharistic celebration.

Critical Reflection on the Present Situation

The Rite seems to be at least partially to blame for the inaction and the confusion that is occurring. Whereas the introduction regarding the other stages of Christian initiation are much more clear about what happens during those periods, those concerning mystagogy are rather sparse. While the 1988 edition contains almost three times as much text as the provisional text regarding mystagogy, the instructions are still rather vague.[13]

The period of the catechumenate and the period of purification and enlightenment include numerous rituals.[14] The only rituals during the period of postbaptismal catechesis or mystagogy are the Sunday Eucharists during the Easter season and a Mass with the bishop. In many parishes, the neophytes have no distinct role in the Sunday Eucharist during the Easter season. Following the intense rituals of Lent and the Triduum, this can be experienced as a ritual letdown.

The academic calendar often has more influence on parish life than the liturgical calendar does. Thus, in many parishes there is a tendency to use both the language and structures of academia in the process of Christian initiation. A number of resources, especially those published immediately after the introduction of the *Rite of Christian Initiation of Adults*, provide a detailed curriculum that can easily give one the impression that the Christian initiation of adults is primarily an educational program.[15] Together with a tendency to see baptism as the goal of initiation, the Easter Vigil can be thought of as a graduation. This kind of understanding can lead one to believe that mystagogy is totally unnecessary, about as important to one's overall education as a class reunion.

J. Michael McMahon reminds us that

> Neither the sacraments of initiation nor their preparation are ends in themselves. They allow believers to enter into a new life, as they are joined to Christ and share with others who have also responded to the proclamation of the good news (85).

Until catechists and others in leadership in the church believe that "the initiation journey never really comes to an end" (McMahon 89), mystagogy will be considered unimportant because the initiation process will have already ended with the reception of the Easter sacraments.

Catechesis, preaching, and ritual celebrations can sometimes focus too narrowly on personal salvation. They can also proclaim a kind of magical understanding of sacraments. These misunderstandings of the tradition can also lead to a notion that salvation is complete once one has been fully initiated. Once complete, there is no need for "deepening the Christian experience, for spiritual growth and for entering more fully into the life and unity of the community" (RCIA 7.4), and thus mystagogy becomes unnecessary.

How particular communities celebrate the early stages of the initiation process can make it difficult to celebrate an effective mystagogy. The signing of the senses during the rite of acceptance into the order of catechumens is often celebrated as if this is simply a ritual blessing. The paradoxical power of the cross as a symbol of both death and life, both blessing and curse is diminished, and the catechumen's experience of the paschal mystery is minimized. The scrutinies are often celebrated as blessings of the Elect (Paris) rather than exorcisms that "uncover, then heal all that is weak, defective, or sinful in the hearts of the Elect" as well as "bring out, then strengthen all that is upright, strong and good" (RCIA 141). A small amount of water poured over the forehead of the Elect can minimize any sense that baptism involves "dying with Christ." When the power of the ritual is not experienced in its fullness, it can prevent, or at least make it difficult for, the neophytes to experience that they have been immersed into the paschal mystery of Christ's dying and rising. When ritual signs are minimized, when the paschal character (RCIA 8) of the process is not evidenced, the mystery that mystagogy reflects on may seem absent, thus making reflection on the mystery almost impossible.

The ways in which the previous periods of Christian initiation are celebrated can become obstacles to an effective mystagogy, obstacles not easily overcome. Mystagogy depends on a period of evangelization during which a person feels "called away from sin and drawn into the mystery of God's love" (RCIA 37). It depends on the period of the catechumenate during which catechumens were led "not only to an appropriate acquaintance with dogmas and precepts but also to a profound sense of the mystery of salvation in which they desire to participate" (RCIA 75.1). It depends on rituals that are real celebrations of God's presence in the world and in the lives of all who believe. It depends on symbols that are lavish and gestures that are strong signs of God's action in our lives. Mystagogy cannot make up for what is lacking in the earlier periods of Christian initiation.

> Mystagogia is the last thing to come and the first thing to fall apart, not just because we are tired but because, in all honesty, we don't know what to do with it and the trivia we fill it with invites boredom. Have we, in the last analysis, brought these people through nine months, a year, two years, or more of intense preparation for entrance into a life about which we have nothing to say? A life with which we are bored or about which we are so ignorant or have so little experience that we have nothing to share? (Hixon 141–142).

The truth is often that we don't have enough experience of the renewed liturgy or ecclesiology of Vatican II to know what to say to neophytes. Members of the Catholic Church baptized in infancy do not know what the experience of the neophytes is really like, and our imaginations are limited by our own experiences or lack of experience of conversion.

On the other hand, some pastoral ministers have had such powerful experiences with the Christian initiation of adults that they believe that it can solve all the problems of the parish. They put all their eggs in this one basket. The Christian initiation of adults is not a renewal program for the parish. It is a ritual process that often engages the faithful in new ways of being a parish, but that is not its primary goal. Those who use it in this way may be misusing it.

Small faith communities are often formed during the initiation process. Catechumens, sponsors, and catechists form strong personal relationships that often disappear shortly after initiation.

> Of all the stages in the RCIA, the mystagogical period perhaps calls for the most change in pastoral practice. If we spend the other periods initiating people into a community of celebration and ministry, that community must stay with them during the Easter season to help them reflect on what has happened and to help them

make decisions for the future.

Even more, I would take the stance that so many values in secularized America conflict with Gospel values that to continue to grow in faith the newly baptized need to have some regular contact with a small prayer community which will also provide support (Dunning, "The Stages of Initiation," 242).

Once initiated into the larger church, the neophyte is often abandoned by both sponsors/godparents and catechists, who have the mistaken impression that once a person is initiated they no longer need the support that was part of their preparation for initiation. It may in fact be that they need the support of the community even more, and that may be why so many neophytes leave the community they have spent so much time preparing to join.

The Christian Story and Vision

In the early church, there was often much that needed to be shared with recent converts to the new way of Christianity. The First Letter of Peter has a postbaptismal character. "Some scholars have seen in 1:3—4:11 a baptismal homily or liturgy, with 1:1–2 and 4:12—5:14 as later additions" (Dalton 904). Today it is used throughout the Easter season as the second reading for the Sundays in cycle A—at what are sometimes called the "Masses for neophytes" (RCIA 25).

By the fourth century, the catechumenal process was highly developed, with specific stages and rites. This included the postbaptismal catechesis or mystagogy.

Preparation for the sacraments did not include explanations of the rites. Instead, the great teaching bishops of this period directed candidates' reflection on God's word and challenged them to shape their lives according to the Gospel. Details about the rites and their meaning were kept secret till after the candidates had experienced them (McMahon 89).

Keeping certain details of Christian worship and belief secret is totally foreign to us, but it must have been completely natural to .

the preachers and people of that time. For a candidate undergoing initiation, experiencing the unknown and learning its meaning were an integral part of becoming members of the church (Jeanes 101).

Generally, mystagogy consisted of daily gatherings of the neophytes and many of the Christian faithful during Easter week. The bishop presided and in his homily led the community in a reflection on the mystery they had recently celebrated—the baptism, chrismation, and first sharing in the Eucharist with the neophytes at Easter. These celebrations were filled with such excitement that Egeria, writing about her experience of the mystagogy in Jerusalem toward the end of the fourth century, stated the following:

> When it is Easter week, during the eight days from Easter Sunday to its octave, as soon as the dismissal has been given from the church, everyone, singing hymns, goes to the Anastasis. Soon a prayer is said, the faithful are blessed, and the bishop stands up. Leaning on the inner railing, which is in the grotto of the Anastasis, he explains everything which is accomplished in baptism. At this hour no catechumen goes into the Anastasis; only the neophytes and the faithful who wish to hear the mysteries enter the Anastasis. Indeed, the doors are closed, lest any catechumen come that way. While the bishop is discussing and explaining each point, so loud are the voices in praise that they can be heard outside the church. And he explains all these mysteries in such a manner that there is no one who would not be drawn to them, when he heard them thus explained (Gingras 125).

Examples of the mystagogical preaching of Zeno of Verona (Jeanes), Ambrose of Milan (Deferrari), Theodore of Mopsuestia (Mingana, *Commentary of Theodore of Mopsuestia on the Lord's Prayer*), John Chrysostom (Harkins), Cyril of Jerusalem (McCauley and Stephenson; Mazza),[16] and Augustine of Hippo (Harmless) are available for our study. They teach us that mystagogy begins with the experience of the sacraments of initiation and seeks to interpret the experience of initiation so that the connections can be seen between liturgy, life, and the traditions of Christianity.

The initiation process developed during the early centuries of Christian history, however, disappeared over the centuries as Christianity spread throughout Europe and the practice of adult baptism was almost entirely replaced by the practice of infant baptism. Likewise, the allegorical and typological methods of the ancient mystagogues were found to be inadequate as both the experience of the church and the philosophical systems of understanding that formed people's worldview changed, developed, and expanded (Fragomeni).

The bishops at Vatican II called the church to reestablish the "catechumenate for adults, divided into several stages" (*Constitution on the Sacred Liturgy* 64).

To plot out this journey, the concilium that drafted the RCIA turned to ancient "maps": to ancient sacramentaries and church orders, to patristic sermons and apologetic works. This was sparked not by some romantic yearning for the archaic. Rather the concilium found in these ancient maps a forgotten wisdom—a theological vision, a psychological sensitivity, a pastoral realism—a wisdom that, despite its antiquity, seemed surprisingly contemporary (Harmless 2).

Thus mystagogy was reintroduced into both the language and practice of the church. A provisional text of the *Rite of Christian Initiation of Adults* was first made available in English in 1974.[17] In 1988 a revised text was approved for use in the United States of America with additional rites for those who are already baptized and seek to complete their full initiation in the Catholic Church. Both the 1974 provisional text and the 1988 complete text call this final period of initiation the period of *postbaptismal catechesis*. In 1974, it was also called *mystagogia*, whereas in the 1988 edition, the word was anglicized as *mystagogy*.

In the Rite itself, the time for mystagogy is "usually the Easter season," the fifty days from Easter to Pentecost. The *National Statutes for the Catechumenate*, however, extends mystagogy "until the anniversary of Christian initiation, with at least monthly assemblies of the neophytes" (24). It seems, therefore, that mystagogy has two distinct time periods—the immediate mystagogy of the Easter season[18] and the extended mystagogy of the first year after the celebration of initiation.

When it comes to mystagogy, the vision of the rite seems clear. Mystagogy takes place primarily in the celebration of the Easter season, especially when the whole community gathers at the Sunday Eucharist (RCIA 7.4, 8, 9.5, 25, 247). It is meant to deepen the experience already begun in the celebration of the Easter sacraments (RCIA 245). It is likewise meant to help the neophytes enter more fully into the life of the local community (RCIA 7.4). It does this through three activities: meditation on the Gospel, sharing the Eucharist, doing the works of charity (RCIA 244). Two of these three activities are not completely new experiences for the neophytes. Meditation on the Gospel has occurred throughout the initiation process, especially during the homilies and the catechesis that followed the dismissals from the Liturgy of the Word. Doing works of charity is also an important part of the period of the catechumenate.[19] While meditation on the Gospel and doing works of charity are not new activities for neophytes, the experience is often changed after initiation. Only the sharing in the Eucharist should be a totally new experience for the neophytes during mystagogy.

> The primary task of Christian initiation is to prepare people for life in the eucharistic community. In the Sunday eucharist the community of faith celebrates the Paschal Mystery of Christ's life, passion, death and resurrection as the paradigm of its own life (Klein 22).

The Rite presumes that parishes are eucharistic communities; some would also say "initiating communities."[20] The vision of the Rite[21] also presumes that parishes are mystagogical communities— communities in which the mysteries are not only celebrated but also appreciated and meditated on, communities in which the mysteries send people forth to continue the mission of Jesus Christ to establish the reign of God here on earth today. Mystagogical communities do not only meditate on the Gospel during the Easter season. They do not only share the Eucharist at the Masses for the neophytes. They do not only engage in acts of charity from Easter until Pentecost or only during the first year of one's membership in the church. Mystagogical communities do all of these things all of the time. In mystagogical communities, the word of God is not only proclaimed and meditated on, it is lived out daily in the lives of the community. In mystagogical communities, people do not need to be reminded that the Sunday Eucharist is a celebration. They celebrate the real presence of Christ in their midst every time two or more of their members are gathered. In mystagogical communities, people don't have to say over and over again, "We are a community." Anyone who looks at the parish can tell it is a community. In mystagogical communities, everyone knows that they are ministers on mission, everyone knows that they have been sent by Christ to proclaim the good news of salvation, everyone knows that "the reign of God is in our midst."

Some Challenges Presented by the Rite and by Present Practices

My experience tells me that many of the parishes that exist in the Catholic Church today are not mystagogical communities. Many aren't even aware that they should be. The challenges of the *Rite of Christian Initiation of Adults* are many. We are challenged to be mystagogical communities, and I am afraid that we are often missing the boat. It may in fact be possible that many of our neophytes are leaving the Sunday assembly, because they have learned to meditate on the Gospel, but they don't see the members of their local parish doing so. They may want to share in the Eucharist, but their experience of the Eucharist has little to do with sharing. They may feel called to do works of charity, but they see few opportunities to do so in their local parish or they see few members of the local parish engaged in such activities.

Other questions arise from the conversation—"the to-and-fro, the back and forth movements" (Tracy 158)—between present practices, the Rite, and myself. They include the following:[22]

- Do our celebrations of the liturgy teach neophytes and others in the church that life, liturgy, and the tradition are connected?

- Do our liturgical practices witness to a church that is all the faithful, not just the clergy and select few who are engaged in ministry?

- Do our liturgical practices indicate that the real presence of Christ exists in the assembly gathered and in the word proclaimed as well as in the bread broken and the wine poured?

- Do our liturgical practices indicate that the sacraments are private or personal celebrations rather than celebrations of the whole community?

- Do our liturgical practices send the assembly forth for mission—for proclaiming the good news of the reign of God, for living the Gospel in their homes and in the marketplace?

- Are our liturgical practices related to our catechetical practices? Do we celebrate what we believe? Are our catechetical practices related to our liturgical practices? Do we believe what we celebrate?[23]

- Do our catechetical practices teach doctrinal formulations or pass on the faith?[24]

- Do our catechetical practices proclaim that Easter is the end of the process or the beginning?

- Do our catechetical practices include the call to mission, to Christian service for the sake of the reign of God?

- Do our catechetical practices take our liturgical experiences seriously? Do they help neophytes and others in the parish reflect on their liturgical experiences and see the connections those experiences have with life and with the Christian tradition?

These questions may affirm or challenge the present liturgical and catechetical practices of a particular community. They may call those in leadership in the local community to set off in new directions. They may help a community reflect on how it might become more and more of a mystagogical community.

In Search of an Effective Mystagogy?

Because my experience, the experience of many others engaged in the ministry of Christian initiation, and the text of the *Rite of Christian Initiation of Adults* offer us so many challenges, I have decided to enter into a search for an effective mystagogy. This book is the result of conversations with both mystagogues and neophytes in several parishes around the country. Their stories and experiences, as well as the preaching of several ancient mystagogues and the challenges presented by the Rite itself, will lead to the creation of an effective mystagogy.

Before describing the method I used in preparing this book, it would be useful to describe what I mean by *effective*, which is so critical to the creation of an *effective* mystagogy. I will first offer a rationale for a process that can be used to evaluate the effectiveness of any formative activity, a process called "behavioral assessment."

> When the RCIA speaks of the process of Christian conversion, it focuses not only on what happens in the catechumens [sic] head and heart but also on the substance of one's daily life. In the final analysis, conversion is about change, and this means that new behaviors are an integral part of what is gradually developing. (Duggan, "Mystagogia and Continuing Conversion," 29).

The initiation process is itself formative, and it is, therefore, appropriate to suggest that behavioral assessment methods can be used to evaluate the effectiveness of mystagogy and postbaptismal catechesis.

While conducting workshops for catechists and liturgical ministers, other members of the diocesan team have often insisted that immediate evaluations of these workshops were essential.[25] While these kinds of evaluations can be helpful, a different criteria to determine the effectiveness of a workshop can also be useful. I ask a simple question, "What difference did it make?" It is a question that cannot be asked immediately after the workshop. Some time needs to pass, a few weeks, a few months, possibly even a few years. "How has your thinking about the topic changed? How has the way in which you minister changed?" These are questions I must also ask myself after a workshop. "How has my thinking changed because of the interaction with these other ministers? How has the way in which I minister changed because of what I said and what I heard?" These are behavioral questions.[26]

Raymond P. Carey trains vocation and formation directors for religious congregations to use a behavioral assessment approach to evaluate candidates who are discerning a call to community life. His approach has both a theological and psychological basis ("Theological and Psychological Perspectives").

> "Behavioral assessment" is an approach for gathering information that has its practical and theoretical roots in an area of clinical psychology called [by] a variety of names: behavior therapy, cognitive-behavior therapy, and/or social learning theory. Behavioral assessment has an interest only in the behaviors and cognitions of a person, and is an approach that looks for *what, when, where and under what circumstances* a person thinks and acts ("Realizing the Vision").

While the behavioral assessment process was originally designed for use in initial assessment of potential candidates, it also has ramifications for the ongoing evaluation processes that are part of any formation program. These evaluations are based on specific behavioral goals and objectives. Using the behavioral assessment model for evaluating a particular community's postbaptismal catechesis or mystagogy, an interviewer would be interested in how the neophytes' experiences correspond to the goals enunciated in the Rite.

The Rite provides some of these behavioral goals for mystagogy when it states the following:

> [Mystagogy] is a time for deepening the Christian experience, for spiritual growth, and for entering more fully into the life and unity of the community (RCIA 7.4).

The faithful should take part in the Masses for neophytes, that is, the Sunday Masses of the Easter season, welcome the neophytes with open arms in charity, and help them to feel at home in the community of the baptized (RCIA 9.5).

[Mystagogy] is a time for the community and the neophytes together to grow in deepening their grasp of the paschal mystery and in making it part of their lives through mediation on the Gospel, sharing in the eucharist, and doing works of charity (RCIA 244).

Some of the following questions might help one discover if these goals are being met:

- Have the recent neophytes experienced mystagogy as a time of deepening their faith and entering more fully into the life of the community?

- Have they felt welcomed into the larger community? More at home in the larger parish?

- Have they come to a fuller understanding of the paschal mystery? Do they recognize the mystery of God's presence in the midst of suffering?

- Have they meditated on the Gospel, shared the Eucharist, and done works of charity?

These questions can only be answered after interviews with the recent neophytes, interviews that include questions like these:

- How has your faith life or spiritual life changed since your initiation into the Christian community at Easter?

- How has your relationship to the local Christian community changed?

- How has your understanding of suffering, redemption, and salvation changed?

- What impact does the Gospel have on your life? Where or how do you reflect on the Gospel's meaning in your life (in the homily, in private meditation, in group reflection, and so on)?

- What impact does your sharing in the Eucharist have on your life? Do you experience communion with God, Christ, and your fellow believers when you share the Eucharist?

- What do you do to spread the good news? Are there some specific ways in which you minister in the world today?

- What specific experiences during mystagogy have had the most impact on you and the ways in which you live your faith?

- What experiences would have helped you feel more like you were part of the Christian community? What experiences would have helped you to have a deeper understanding of what occurred at the Easter Vigil and what occurs every Sunday? What experiences would have helped you to be a more faithful Christian?

If there is no behavioral evidence that anything has changed in the lives of the neophytes since their initiation, it would be difficult to consider mystagogy effective. If the neophytes describe their spiritual lives as personal relationships with the Lord Jesus but without much of a sense of being part of a larger community of faith, it would be difficult to conclude that an adequate sense of unity within the Christian community exists. If, however, a deepening sense of God's presence in their lives occurs; if they have experiences of being more closely united to their fellow believers; if they see themselves as ministers of the reign of God, then clearly something is happening in their lives that could be considered effective. Effective mystagogy is ultimately the result of God's actions, but the mystagogue and the Christian community provide opportunities for the neophytes to experience the actions of God in their lives and in the lives of the whole community. Good mystagogical experiences foster and nourish faith. Poor ones may weaken and destroy it.[27]

Once the effectiveness of the postbaptismal catechesis and mystagogy of a particular community has been evaluated, a description of that process might be helpful in designing a mystagogy that is effective for other people from similar cultural backgrounds. This is, in effect, the goal of this book.

A Mystagogical Method

The fourth-century mystagogues used a method of preaching that took the liturgical experience of what today we call the Easter Vigil as its starting point. As they preached during the week after Easter, the mystagogues reminded the neophytes and all who had gathered for mystagogy of that experience of symbols, gestures, and words that were part of the experience of initiation. By their preaching, they helped the assembly reflect on the experience and shared with them parts of the Christian tradition, especially as found in the Hebrew Scriptures and in the writings of the apostles. Using allegory and typology, they helped the neophytes and the rest of the assembly recognize how their experience was related to the larger story of salvation. They saw as their purpose "to give the baptized the understanding and motivation that will enable them to live the life in Christ that has been bestowed in them in the liturgical celebration" (Mazza 165).

A similar method is used today by some who do ritual catechesis. The focus of their catechesis is the celebration of a particular rite. The symbols, gestures, words, and Scriptures of that ritual are remembered and reflected on. The whole experience is analyzed for its deeper meaning(s). The catechist helps those who experienced the rite to recall and to name the thoughts, feelings, and sensations that were part of their experience. The catechist likewise helps them recognize in their own experiences the presence of God and relates their experiences to the experiences of others in the tradition. Sharing the stories of Scripture, history, and teachings from both the past and present, the catechist helps them recognize that their experiences are part of something that has a long history, that has occurred in many ways in the lives of many people. Those who celebrate a particular liturgical rite enter into a dialogue between their own experience and the experiences of ages past and yet to come. They recognize that they are part of something far bigger than that one ritual and this one community. They see connections between their own lives, the lives of the saints who have come before them, and those who are yet to be born. The final step in this method of ritual catechesis is for the catechist to ask each of those present to reflect on one concrete action they might take in response to the action that God has taken in them and then to pray for one another that all may have the grace needed to respond to God's blessings.

The method of the fourth-century mystagogues and that of contemporary liturgical catechists have many similarities. They both follow a pattern that Thomas H. Groome has called shared Christian praxis. His method begins with a focusing activity that sets the stage for the teaching/learning that follows. This is followed by the first movement, in which participants are invited "to 'name' or express in some form their own and/or society's 'present action,' … [to] depict how the theme is being lived or produced, dealt with or realized, 'going on' or 'being done' in their own or society's praxis" (Groome 146). In movement two, the participants engage in critical reflection concerning the "present action" expressed in the first movement. Any and all kinds of analysis and critical reflection techniques can be part of this movement. During the third movement, the Christian tradition is shared around the theme(s) or symbol(s) that have been the focus from the beginning. Groome calls this "Making Accessible the Christian Story/Vision." In the fourth movement, "participants ask, 'How does this Christian Story/Vision affirm, question, and call us beyond present praxis?' And conversely, 'How does present praxis affirm and critically appropriate the version of Story/Vision made accessible in movement 3, and how are we to live more faithfully toward the Vision of God's reign?'" (Groome 147). The fifth and final movement calls the participants to a decision or response for "Lived Christian Faith." It invites the participants to ask themselves, "What are we going to do about what we've done in the previous movements?"

These three methods, similar in their process, are also the method of this book, a method already anticipated in this introduction. The divisions of this introduction and the chapters of this book follow this method. The introduction focuses us on the topic at hand. It gives us a common experience from which to reflect on what follows. Susan's story focuses on the topic at hand. The section The Experience of Mystagogy in the Church in the United States of America names some of what is happening with mystagogy today. The next section takes a critical look at the current situation. The fourth-century mystagogues and the Rite are explored as a sharing of The Christian Story and Vision. The next section, Some Challenges Presented by the Rite and Present Practices, seeks to answer the question, "What challenges does the history and Rite offer to our present practice of mystagogy?" In response to all these challenges, I have decided to begin a journey in search of an effective mystagogy. What is meant by "effective" and what methods will be used in this search are part of this final section, which leads us off on the search again.

In the first chapter of this book, I will describe the initiatory practices of several parishes. In the second chapter, I will seek to analyze these practices from several points of view. Among them will be responses from the perspectives of recent neophytes and the mystagogues in their communities. In chapter 3, I will seek to expand The Christian Story and Vision already presented in the introduction, delving deeper into both the fourth century and the contemporary Rite. In chapter 4, I will establish a dialogue between the tradition and the present practices already investigated. I will seek to answer the question, "How does our tradition affirm and challenge our present initiatory practices?" Finally, in chapter 5, I will offer some specific suggestions for a contemporary mystagogical practice based on all that has come before.

Not only do the chapters of this book follow the shared Christian praxis method, the project itself was an experience of shared Christian praxis. In fact, one might say it was two such experiences. The first began with my own experiences and some of the present practices described in some of the recent literature concerning mystagogy. The second will begin with the interviews and conversations with recent neophytes and mystagogues in the parishes that are part of this project. In both cases, there was critical reflection on the present practices and experiences, a sharing of the Christian story/vision, followed by a conversation in which the present practices and the

Christian story/vision both affirmed and challenged one another. In the first experience, the decision was to search for an effective mystagogy by examining what was actually happening in three different parishes. In the second, the response was to suggest what could be done in the future, not only in those parishes but also in others who are struggling to create an effective mystagogy for their neophytes. This introduction is the written record of the first experience of shared Christian praxis concerning mystagogy. The rest of this book is the second.

It is my firm belief that the method of shared Christian praxis is itself mystagogical, for it begins with experience, and it is in our experiences that God has and continues to reveal Godself to the world.

Thomas H. Groome's Shared Christian Praxis	Parts of this Introduction	The Chapters in this Book	The Method of the Fourth-Century Mystagogues	A Method for Ritual Catechesis Today
Focusing Activity	My Experience with Mystagogy	Introduction: Focusing on Mystagogy	For the ancient mystagogues, the celebration of the Easter Vigil and readings from the Scriptures during the octave of Easter are the focus for the homily.	The celebration of one of the rites and the celebration of the word that begins the catechesis are the focus for the catechetical session.
Movement 1: Naming/Expressing "Present Action"	The Experience of Mystagogy in the Church in the United States of America	Chapter 1: Present Mystagogical Practices in Three Parishes	In the homily, the ancient mystagogues reminded the neophytes and all who were assembled of an experience that was part of the Easter Vigil celebration.	In the catechetical session, the mystagogue reminds the neophytes and all who are gathered of an experience that was part of the rite that had been celebrated.
Movement 2: Critical Reflection on Present Action	Critical Reflection on the Present Situation	Chapter 2: Analysis of the Present Practices	As part of the homily, the mystagogue reflected with the assembly on the experience.	In the catechetical session, the mystagogue invites the neophytes and all who are gathered to share how they experienced what happened during the ritual.
Movement 3: Making Accessible the Christian Story/Vision	The Christian Story and Vision	Chapter 3: The Church's Vision of Mystagogy	The mystagogue shared parts of the Christian story/vision, especially as found in the Hebrew Scriptures but also as found in the apostolic writings.	The mystagogue shares parts of the Christian story/vision found in the Scriptures, especially the Christian Scriptures, and the historical and doctrinal traditions of the church.
Movement 4: Dialectical Hermeneutics to Appropriate the Story/Vision to the Participants' Stories/Visions	Some Challenges Presented by the Rite and Present Practices	Chapter 4: A Conversation with Present Practices and the Church's Vision of Mystagogy	The mystagogue used allegory and typology to help the neophytes and the assembly integrate their experience with the larger Christian story/vision.	The mystagogue, the neophytes, and those gathered enter into a dialogue that helps them make connections between their ritual experience, their life experience, and the Christian tradition.
Movement 5: Decision/Response for Lived Christian Faith	In Search of an Effective Mystagogy?	Chapter 5: Suggestions for a Contemporary Mystagogical Practice	The mystagogue often encouraged and challenged the neophytes and the whole community to live the Christian life in accord with what they heard and experienced. The neophytes were prayed for in a liturgical setting.	The mystagogue often asks the neophytes and others gathered to reflect on and name some concrete action they will take to live out what they have learned from the ritual they have experienced. All offer prayers for one another as they seek to meet the challenges of living the Christian faith.

Chapter 1

Present Mystagogical Practices in Three Parishes

This search for an effective mystagogy began with conversations with several colleagues[1] who suggested five parishes where they believed an effective mystagogy was already in place.[2] I followed up with conversations with eighteen neophytes and twelve mystagogues from these five parishes in three dioceses in the United States. I started not with theory but with the actual practices of mystagogy, not with an empirical sampling of the experiences of neophytes and mystagogues in the United States, but with the stories shared by thirty specific neophytes and mystagogues. Their names, and the names of the parishes where they experienced the Christian initiation of adults, have been changed to ensure confidentiality, but their stories are *their* stories.[3] The descriptions that follow are based on their descriptions of their experiences.

St. Ambrose of Milan Parish: Archdiocese of St. Paul and Minneapolis

At St. Ambrose Parish, I met with the director of adult and sacramental education, one convert, and three members of the parish initiation team.[4] All of the members of the initiation team were catechists throughout the initiation process and therefore, mystagogues as well. Two of the catechists and the convert had also served as sponsors. The convert could hardly be called a neophyte, having been initiated five years prior to our discussions. Our discussions, however, painted the following picture of the parish and the initiation process that takes place there.

27

General Description of the Parish[5]

St. Ambrose of Milan Parish was established as suburbs began to expand at the end of World War II. About half the parish members have been lifelong members of the community, with about 20 percent of the members moving into the community within the past five years. Most parishioners are middle class European Americans with a high school education. A number of Korean and Vietnamese families have recently joined the community as well.

The church building is contemporary, built within the last thirty years, with a large square baptismal font near the main entry to the assembly space. It has flowing water and is large enough for immersion of adults. There is a large gathering space where ministers of hospitality welcome the community and where they gather after liturgy for food and fellowship. The assembly space is arranged so that four seating sections form a semicircle around the sanctuary.

The assembly seems to be engaged in the liturgy. They actively participate in the responses and songs. Both contemporary and more traditional music styles are employed. Body language indicates an attentiveness to the word as it is proclaimed and to the preaching of the homily. People seem friendly and greet each other both before liturgy and at the sign of peace. Almost everyone shares in communion, with about half sharing from the cup as well as the bread. Between 10 and 20 percent of the assembly participates in fellowship after the service in the parish gathering space.

The parish sponsors a grade school and religious education programs for both children and adults.

The St. Ambrose of Milan Parish staff includes the following positions:

- pastor (diocesan priest)

- weekend associate pastor (religious priest)

- two permanent deacons

- pastoral minister (religious woman)

28

- liturgical music director and assistant director

- director of adult and sacramental education

- director of Sunday School, elementary religious education and religious education for unique learners

- coordinator for youth ministry

- business administrator

- bookkeeper

- school principal and administrative assistant

- parish and religious education secretaries[6]

The parish seems quite active, with numerous programs in religious education and social outreach. There is an obvious care and concern about the liturgical life of the parish community as well.

Description of the RCIA at St. Ambrose Parish

The director of adult and sacramental education coordinates the implementation of the *Rite of Christian Initiation of Adults*. She is assisted by a team of five volunteers from the parish. The director and some of the team have attended workshops sponsored by the Archdiocese of St. Paul and Minneapolis, as well as the Second International Convocation of the North American Forum on the Catechumenate (which was held in Minneapolis in 1993). The director has also attended a Liturgies Institute and a Remembering Church Institute sponsored by the North American Forum on the Catechumenate.

St. Ambrose Parish has implemented the Rite for the past ten years, following a school-year model, which begins with inquiry meetings in early September.[7] Prior to the first meeting of the inquirers, the director meets individually with each inquirer to gather information, answer questions, and offer a brief outline of the initiation process.

Inquirers gather on Thursday evenings for about two hours. Members of the initiation team facilitate discussions that focus on the questions of the inquirers as well as on the proclamation of the good news of Jesus Christ. During the period of inquiry, sponsors are assigned by the parish team to each of the inquirers. After about two months of inquiry, the inquirers are invited to a discernment retreat, as they prepare to celebrate the rite of acceptance.[8] This celebration takes place once a year on either the Feast of Christ the King or the Second Sunday of Advent. While distinctions are made between catechumens and candidates for full communion during the rituals, no distinctions are made regarding catechesis during any of the periods of the Christian initiation of adults. Catechumens and candidates are dismissed from the Sunday assembly whenever rituals from the *Rite of Christian Initiation of Adults* are celebrated.[9]

Catechumens and candidates for full communion continue to meet with the sponsors and catechists on Thursday evenings throughout the period of the catechumenate. These catechetical sessions begin with reflection on the readings from the previous Sunday's liturgy. The content of the catechetical session is drawn from the catechist's reflections on the Gospel from the previous Sunday and the questions that arise from the reflections of the catechumens and candidates.

A second discernment retreat is held prior to the beginning of Lent. Catechumens and candidates who believe they are ready to continue toward baptism or full communion in the Catholic Church[10] are invited to celebrate the rite of sending (at the parish)[11] and the rite of election (at the cathedral)[12] on the First Sunday of Lent.

During Lent, the penitential rite is celebrated on the Second Sunday of Lent for the candidates for full communion. The scrutinies are celebrated with the Elect on the Third, Fourth, and Fifth Sundays of Lent at one of the parish liturgies. Dismissals take place after each of these rituals. Children and adults among the Elect and the candidates participate in these rites together. This past year, these rites were so powerful that several parishioners complained that they felt "like exorcisms."

Catechesis during Lent consists of reflections on the word of God after the dismissals from the Sunday liturgies, brief preparations for the rituals at the end of each dismissal session, and gatherings as part of small faith-sharing groups each week.[13] During Lent, the Elect and the candidates for full communion often "express a longing or desire for the eucharist." A morning of prayer and reflection takes place on Holy Saturday as part of the immediate preparation for the Easter Vigil. These preparations include a rehearsal of the Easter Vigil[14] and the celebration of the Ephphetha Rite (RCIA 197–198).

Mystagogy at St. Ambrose Parish

Once they have completed their initiation at the Easter Vigil, the neophytes are invited to come together on Thursday evenings for mystagogy. Mystagogy at St. Ambrose Parish begins with Easter and concludes just prior to Pentecost.

The following questions set the agenda for the first gathering during mystagogy:

What did you see? What did you hear? What did you experience? What did you feel? Taste? What does it mean?

By then these questions have already "become a mantra." Neophytes have already reflected on the questions after each of the previous ritual celebrations,[15] so that when they gather for the first time after the celebration of the sacraments of initiation they immediately began to share their experiences "not only of the Easter Vigil, but also of the Triduum."

During mystagogy, the neophytes, their sponsors, and the parish mystagogues gather four or five times. One evening during mystagogy, "ministers from the parish let neophytes know what ministries are available to them." They also hear the witness of one of the catechists who is also a Maryknoll lay missionary. Her witness concerning her experience of ministry in Guatemala is meant to encourage the neophytes to find ways to minister to others as a response to their experience of initiation.

Because the parish choir rehearses at the same time that catechesis for the Christian initiation of adults takes place, choir members invite the catechumens, candidates, and sponsors to join them in the church for prayer. During mystagogy, the roles are reversed, and the neophytes host the choir members in the gathering space where they usually meet.

A picnic with the neophytes, sponsors, mystagogues, and their families takes place toward the end of the Easter season. This is the final celebration and gathering of mystagogy at St. Ambrose of Milan Parish.

Some of the sponsors and neophytes are invited to witness about their experience at the Sunday Eucharist on one of the weekends in June. Members of the initiation team indicated that the motives for this witness are (1) to encourage those who may be thinking about becoming Catholic Christians to enter the initiation process; and (2) to recruit parish members as future sponsors. Bulletin announcements are also used for these purposes, and the initiation process begins again at St. Ambrose of Milan Parish.

The Interviews

The director of Christian initiation indicated that most of those who participate in the initiation process are young people (twenty to thirty-five) preparing for marriage or recently married to a Catholic Christian. She stated that between six and eight of every ten of those who complete the initiation process continue to be active members of the parish. She likewise indicated that while some changes had been made over the years, the initiation process at St. Ambrose Parish had basically been the same for the previous ten years. She and the members of the parish initiation team indicated that they had never investigated the possibilities of changing to an ongoing process rather than the school-year model with which they were familiar.

One of the sponsors commented that she had not seen the woman she sponsored the previous year since her baptism. In reflecting on that, she said she thought that the sponsors' role for adults ended with initiation, whereas for children, it began there. She also stated that "sponsors often get more out of [the initiation process] than those they sponsor."

In a separate interview, the convert from St. Ambrose Parish described how important his relationship with his sponsor continues to be. He spoke about how his relationship with his then fiancée (now his wife) continues to foster his own spiritual development as well as his ministerial participation in the life of the parish community.

Over and over again, he spoke about his feelings of being "welcomed," of being "at home here" in St. Ambrose Parish, of being "real comfortable here." He once said, "I'd been searching for a spiritual home ... and I felt pretty confident that I found it here. ... I cannot think of not being here." This relationship to the parish has led him to involvement in several parish ministries—as a sponsor in the initiation process, as a minister of hospitality, and as a facilitator in the parish marriage preparation program.

He likewise described how his initiation influenced his life beyond the parish. He said that "about halfway through the process" he had "a kind of awakening." His new faith forced him to look at his career in new ways, eventually leading him to leave his job and ultimately form his own company. His employees, he said, would say that he tries "to do the Christian thing."

St. Cyril of Jerusalem Parish: Archdiocese of St. Paul and Minneapolis

I met with the pastoral associate of adult formation and RCIA, two other members of the parish initiation team, one neophyte, and four people who were received into the full communion of the Catholic Church through the initiation process at St. Cyril of Jerusalem Parish. I met with each of them separately, except the two members of the parish initiation team who met with me together. They serve as catechists throughout the initiation process, from the period of inquiry through the initial phase of mystagogy that ends at Pentecost in this parish. I also had brief telephone conversations with two neophytes who were unable to meet with me in person but who shared some of their experiences with me. I likewise had the opportunity to meet the pastor and parochial vicar, attended a weekend liturgy, and presided and preached at a holy day liturgy while the parish staff was away for a day of recollection. From these various encounters, the following pictures of St. Cyril Parish arise.

General Description of the Parish

St. Cyril of Jerusalem Parish was established twenty years ago as the suburbs around Minneapolis and St. Paul began to experience phenomenal growth. About three thousand families are registered in the parish. Of those, about 30 percent of the parish membership had lived in the area when the parish was established, having been members of the original parish that was divided to create St. Cyril's. More than 50 percent of the parishioners have lived in the area for less than five years.

Most of the parishioners are European Americans and are under forty-five years old. There are, however, a number of African-American, Asian, and Hispanic families who belong to St. Cyril Parish. Most parishioners are middle to upper-middle class with a college education.

The entire parish is less than ten years old. A large glass-fronted lobby welcomes people to the parish complex. The worship space is central to the structure with offices to one side and meeting rooms and parish hall to the other.

A square submersion[16] baptismal font stands in the entryway of the worship space. The worship space is rectangular, seating about fifteen hundred persons. The sanctuary is located front and center along the long side of the rectangle with six seating areas for the assembly. Large clear windows reach from the floor to the ceiling on either side of the sanctuary, bringing the wooded area around the church property into the worship space. Large ficus and other live plants also bring life to the space.

People seem genuinely friendly toward one another. Though the assembly is quite large, people greet one another and seem to recognize fellow parishioners. During the liturgy, members of the assembly participate in both the sung and recited responses. The music director seems to favor a contemporary style of music with piano, flute, and other instruments as part of a small ensemble.[17] Both priests are described by those I talked to as very good preachers and presiders. Members of the assembly seem genuinely engaged. Several of the neophytes and those received into full communion said that they felt right at home the very first time they worshiped at St. Cyril of Jerusalem Parish.

In addition to the pastor and parochial vicar, there are eleven full or part-time pastoral associates. They include pastoral associates for the following areas:[18]

- Adult Formation and RCIA

- Business Administration

- Family Faith Formation

- Liturgical Music

- Liturgy and Sacramental Preparation

- Preschool

- Pastoral Care

- Shared Ministry (Volunteers)

- Social Justice

- Youth Ministries

In addition to the parish council, the parish bulletin lists the following committees, which coordinate the various ministries of the parish:

- Development Committee

- Faith Formation Committee

- Finance Committee

- Liturgy Committee

- Parish Activities Committee

- Pastoral Committee

- Property Committee

- Shared Ministry Committee

- Social Justice Committee

- Stewardship Committee

Many people at St. Cyril Parish are engaged in some form of church-sponsored ministry. The leadership of the parish seems concerned about the quality of the liturgical life and the social outreach of the community. Several of the ministries at St. Cyril's reach across denominational lines, providing a witness of ecumenical cooperation.

The parish has, in recent years, placed an emphasis on adult formation, especially through the establishment of small Christian communities. Religious education for children is organized by family clusters rather than the traditional school or C.C.D. models. There is no parish school, though tuition assistance is offered to families with children in the schools of two neighboring Catholic parishes.

Description of the RCIA at St. Cyril Parish

The various aspects of the Christian initiation of adults are coordinated by the pastoral associate for adult formation and RCIA.[19] She is assisted by eight volunteers who serve in various capacities as catechists, prayer leaders, and "persons responsible for sponsors, faith sharers, and prayer companions."[20] Members of the initiation team have participated in training programs sponsored by the Archdiocese of St. Paul and Minneapolis, the North American Forum on the Catechumenate, and a local university's graduate program in religious studies. The pastoral associate for adult formation and RCIA also plans training experiences for the other members of the team.

St. Cyril Parish began to implement the *Rite of Christian Initiation of Adults* when it hired the current pastoral associate for adult formation in 1986. Like St. Ambrose Parish, they follow a school-year model of adult initiation, beginning the period of evangelization in early September and the catechumenate in mid-November.[21] The period of purification and enlightenment corresponds with Lent, and formal gathering for mystagogy with the Easter season.

Inquirers gather on Tuesday evenings at the parish complex in a room designed and furnished for adult programs.[22] Each session begins with a focus question about the inquirers' personal experiences of God. They are invited to keep a journal, sharing whatever they feel comfortable sharing with others gathered at tables of six to eight people. Potential sponsors, who have attended a training workshop for sponsors, begin gathering with this group from the beginning. As the weeks pass, inquirers and sponsors are paired up by the sponsor coordinator. Questions, presentations, and discussions are focused on both questions from the inquirers and topics the parish team believe are relevant to an initial evangelization of the actual inquirers who are part of the group.

Each inquirer meets individually with a member of the parish initiation team for discussion and discernment about continuing the process. Those who choose to continue are invited to celebrate the rite of acceptance[23] at one of two Sunday liturgies held on the same day in early or mid-November. The baptismal status of each candidate is respected throughout the rite, with distinct questions and placement in the midst of the assembly.[24] However, there are no distinctions made between those who are baptized and those who are not baptized during any of the catechesis throughout the process.

Each Sunday during the catechumenate, both catechumens and candidates for full communion are dismissed from the main worship service. One catechist accompanies them as they reflect on the Gospel of the day. Those who are unable to attend the regular Tuesday evening catechetical session remain for an additional hour of catechesis on Sunday mornings. This group seems to be considered the exception, with less personnel resources available as catechists and only the occasional participation of the professional staff of the parish. The "regular" group meets on Tuesday evening for about two hours of prayer, catechesis, conversation, and faith sharing.[25] As Lent approaches, sponsors and candidates meet together for a discernment process, after which the sponsors meet individually with a member of the initiation team and "tell them why they think their candidate is ready" to celebrate the rite of election[26] on the First Sunday of Lent.

During Lent, the three scrutinies are celebrated at the main parish liturgy on the Third, Fourth, and Fifth Sundays. Only the unbaptized are scrutinized. The optional scrutiny for the already baptized is not celebrated.[27] A special daylong retreat is held on the day before Palm Sunday. The focus of this retreat is reconciliation, and those who are already baptized are invited to celebrate the sacrament of penance as part of the retreat experience.

From the very beginning of the process, candidates are aware that the process does not end with the celebration of the sacraments of initiation at the Easter Vigil. They are encouraged to continue to meet on Tuesday evenings during the Easter season. *Ninety Days* (Hinman Powell and Sinwell)[28] is used as a primary resource for the catechists who serve as mystagogues during the Easter season. Neophytes and those received into the full communion of the Catholic Church also hear from several parishioners about opportunities for ministry in the local community. They likewise spend time planning and preparing for a celebration of the Eucharist for themselves, their sponsors, and families. This formal period of mystagogy ends with a picnic just before Pentecost.

Many sponsors do not participate in mystagogy: "It's almost like, now that they're Catholic, I don't have to be with them." Mystagogy continues, with an invitation from the pastoral associate for adult formation and RCIA to form a small Christian community.[29] Mystagogy is the least formal of the periods during the initiation process. The director said, "Mystagogy is really all about continuing your life in the community—not these formal sessions."

The Interviews

The pastoral associate for adult formation and RCIA expressed interest in moving to a year-round model of initiation, where the precatechumenate and the catechumenate are ongoing whenever there are inquirers and catechumens in the parish, regardless of the time of the year.[30] She, however, expressed some doubts as to whether it would be possible to implement the process in this way given the constraints of time and volunteer personnel available at St. Cyril's.

Over the past three years, the average number of adult converts has been three, with eleven or twelve adults received into the full communion of the Catholic Church each year. All of those I interviewed continued to participate in the life of the parish after their initiation. All of them had regularly participated in the liturgical life of the parish prior to their participation in the initiation process. It seemed, though I cannot be certain, that those few who did not participate in the life of the parish prior to their full initiation in the church returned to that pattern after the Easter Vigil.[31]

Each of the neophytes and those received into the full communion of the Catholic Church described how the experience of sharing their faith with one another had changed their lives. They made statements such as the following:

> I appreciate my husband more ... I think I'm a better person .... There's a clearer picture of [God] .... I'm not afraid to die .... I feel so at peace .... I try to see people like God sees them .... I try to be nicer to people ..... I make that extra effort. ... I feel happier .... I feel more complete.

> [My husband's] beliefs and his values changed me—I started to see things differently—through his eyes .... I'm trying to live my life differently .... God is in everybody and you need to treat everybody like God .... We have to treat everybody that way .... How I treat other people [has certainly changed].

> It's made me and my son a lot closer .... There was even some reconciliation with my ex-wife .... A few years ago I wouldn't have done this.

> [We're] trying to be more understanding of our differences .... We feel closer .... There is more of an understanding of our love and our relationship.

> The way I look at myself changed, because I finally saw a path that God was making for me. So the way I look at myself changed. Some things opened up in my family .... I look at [my sister—who suffered a great personal trauma] a little differently now .... I think I understand my brother [a recovering alcoholic] differently .... Before I just worked—now it's a ministry.

Each of them described how the initiation process influenced personal relationships with themselves, with others, with God. Three of them described how they had or were in the process of reevaluating their careers in light of their faith.

Belonging to a faith community was important to each of them. They used phrases such as these:

I knew I was home.

I felt at home here .... I just long to be here .... I got connected.

I just felt like this was the place for me. I was fighting it the whole way and finally gave in and said, "I belong here." ... These are good people. I want to be part of it ... it's a lifestyle, a sense of community .... I feel like now I belong .... I feel like I can hold my head up .... I know people.

Each of those interviewed described some form of ministry they became involved in as a result of the initiation process. One works in a food pantry, one answers the phones at the parish offices, another is part of a social justice organization. All have become involved in one way or another in living out their newfound faith.

The experience of the rites was described using words such as these:

overwhelmed

the most memorable experience of my adult life. ... Each rite left you longing for more. I felt closer and closer and closer to God all the time .... All the rites were very meaningful. I just couldn't wait to get to the next one. ...

more feeling than I expected

The participation of faith sharers and prayer partners were described as significant, as were the gatherings after dismissals for the catechumens and candidates for full communion.

Each described their experience of mystagogy as a positive experience. They said the following:

> We couldn't wait to talk to each other, to share .... I felt extremely depressed, because I wanted to share right away.

> I'm glad we didn't just quit after Easter .... I realized I still have a lot more to learn.

One was disappointed that many of the sponsors and some of the neophytes and those received into the full communion of the Catholic Church did not continue to gather together after Easter. She said this:

> Half the people didn't show up anymore. It was like Easter came, they got what they needed, that was it. [I wanted to say to them,] "Come on guys, it's not just like going to the movies—you get your experience and you're done. This is something you're suppose to keep going with now. Remember, this is part of your life now. What happened?"

She was also delighted that so many of the neophytes came to the initial meeting to form a small Christian community and felt the need to continue to grow in their faith, as well as in their relationships with one another. Several others had similar feelings.

Two of those interviewed had begun the initiation process once before in other parishes. Both described their first experiences as primarily focused on the education. There were a series of classes—lectures, generally given by one of the priests on the parish staff—with little or no participation by other laypeople. Their previous experiences lacked any ritual celebrations prior to baptism or reception into the full communion. In both cases, there was an emphasis on knowledge of the faith but no witness by others or experience of belonging to a community. Looking back, both described these as major reasons for not completing the process as well as their hesitancy to begin the process again in a new environment. The ritual element, the personal witness, and the participation by many members of the faith community were important aspects of the experience for these two persons.

St. John Chrysostom Parish: Archdiocese of Cincinnati

I met the consultant for catechist formation[32] at St. John Chrysostom Parish while attending a conference on the future of the sacrament of reconciliation. During one of our conversations she asked me what I was working on and volunteered her parish as one that she believed might have an effective mystagogy. Almost a year later I visited the parish and had the opportunity to interview the director of adult initiation and four neophytes. I also had brief conversations with the pastor and the pastor emeritus.

During my visit, I attended a Sunday celebration of the Eucharist, witnessed the dismissal of the catechumens, and joined them, their sponsors, and one of the parish catechists for a catechetical session during the catechumenate. There I encountered catechumens, candidates, and sponsors, and I had brief conversations with several of them about their experience of the initiation process up to that point.

General Description of the Parish

St. John Chrysostom Parish was established shortly after the turn of the century in an urban area of the Cincinnati Archdiocese that was recently settled by German and Irish immigrants to the United States. Always a neighborhood parish, small numbers of immigrants from other nations have also joined the community.[33] Today about fourteen hundred families are registered in the parish. Like the neighborhood in which it is located, most of the parishioners would be considered middle to lower-middle class, families of blue-collar workers. Some 85 percent of the people have always lived in this area of the city, which has a population that is more than 80 percent Roman Catholic. Thus, the population of both the neighborhood and the parish is rather stable.

The church building is Romanesque in style, with high vaulted ceilings, murals, statues, marble altars, and a marble communion railing. The parish had just completed a major restoration of some of the art and architectural structures of the church building. This included a new altar more in line with the architectural style of the church than the previous altar had been.

There is no permanent baptismal font in the church. A large bowl on a stand surrounded by live plants and the Easter candle are located in the center of the central aisle. The font is prominent but clearly temporary. It is suitable only for baptism by infusion, though a newborn infant might be able to be baptized by immersion.[34] At Easter, I am told, a different temporary font, made from plastic and designed to be used as a small pond in landscaping, is used. The presider stands in the water while each candidate kneels in the font and is baptized by immersion.

St. John Chrysostom Parish sponsors a parochial elementary school: preschool through eighth grade. The parish staff includes the following:

- three diocesan priests:

  - the pastor
  - the pastor emeritus
  - priest in residence[35]

- permanent deacon

- two pastoral ministers (religious women)

  - one for adult spiritual formation
  - the other for ministry to the elderly and bereaved

- school principal

- liturgical music director

- business manager

- consultant for catechist formation (religious woman)

Numerous volunteers assist the staff in offering opportunities for religious formation and community outreach through the following programs:

- Advent and Lenten Programs for Adult Formation

    - Breaking Open the Word Sessions[36]
    - Evensong and Speakers Series

- C.C.D.

- Little Rock Scripture Study[37]

- Network of Care[38]

- New Visions Ministry[39]

- Preschool C.C.D.

- Re-membering Church[40]

- Rite of Christian Initiation of Adults

- St. Vincent de Paul Society[41]

The spiritual formation of both children and adults seems to be a major concern of the pastoral staff at St. John Chrysostom Parish, as is the quality of the liturgical life of the community.

Description of the RCIA at St. John Chrysostom Parish

The implementation of the *Rite of Christian Initiation of Adults* is coordinated by the director of adult initiation, who volunteers her time and talent in this position. She coordinates the activities of seven other ministers who have responsibilities for hospitality, catechesis, mystagogy, sponsors, and the Christian initiation of children. She has just completed her first year in this position.

The director of initiation is assisted by the consultant for catechist formation, a religious woman who shares her experience and expertise both as a catechist and in the training and coordinating of the ministry of the catechists who minister in the period of inquiry, the catechumenate, and mystagogy. The pastor also participates in the process as both a catechist and spiritual director in addition to preaching and presiding at the various celebrations of the Rite. Both the pastor and the consultant for catechist formation meet individually with the catechumens and candidates, helping them in their discernment prior to the various celebrations. Additionally, both are presenters at institutes sponsored by the North American Forum on the Catechumenate for the training of ministers of the initiation process.

The director of adult initiation and other members of the initiation team have attended both a Beginnings and Beyond Institute, sponsored by the North American Forum on the Catechumenate, as well as other workshops offered by the archdiocese. The consultant for catechist formation also offers both support and continuing formation to the various members of the initiation team.

The process described in the next few pages is rather new to this parish. St. John Chrysostom Parish recently moved from the school-year model to the year-round model.

When a person expresses some interest in the possibility of becoming a Catholic Christian, the director of adult initiation meets with that person. This conversation is meant to be both welcoming and informational. A general description of the initiation process and an initial assessment of the person's needs are part of this interview. If appropriate, the director invites the person to participate in the weekly inquiry sessions held in the parish center (formerly a convent). She likewise gives each person several pamphlets that both explain the initiation process and introduce them to Catholic practices and beliefs.[42]

The period of inquiry is ongoing; that is, inquiry sessions are held every week throughout the year. Two married couples facilitate these gatherings. The inquirers' questions are the agenda for these gatherings. Beginning with prayer and Scripture, the sessions last about an hour to an hour and a half. The Scripture readings are often chosen because the facilitators believe that they will trigger questions in these particular inquirers. Numerous resources, including *Come Follow Me* (Sinwell), are available to assist the facilitators as they plan these gatherings. The director of adult initiation and the sponsor coordinator also attend many of these sessions to both support the inquirers and come to know them and their needs, as the sponsor coordinator seeks to find the appropriate persons to become each inquirer's sponsor.

Once an inquirer has shown signs of initial conversion, the inquirer is invited to discern whether it is the appropriate time to celebrate the rite of acceptance into the order of catechumens.[43] The inquirer meets with the pastor or the consultant for catechist formation for this discernment. Generally, the rite of acceptance and the right of welcoming the candidates is celebrated three times each year. By this time the inquirer will already have a sponsor who has been appointed by the parish to walk through the initiation process with him or her. Likewise, each catechumen or candidate has a prayer sponsor.[44]

The rite of acceptance begins with the inquirers gathered outside the front doors of the church on a large porch. After some introductory remarks by the presider, the entire assembly processes outside, surrounding the inquirers and then bringing them into the church after they have been welcomed and signed with the sign of the cross.

After celebrating this first ritual during the initiation process, catechumens are dismissed from the Sunday assembly every Sunday until the celebration of the sacraments of initiation. At St. John Chrysostom Parish, the candidates for full communion are invites to be part of the dismissal as well. After the homily, the presider invites the catechumens and those candidates who wish to be dismissed to stand. A short prayer is said as the entire assembly extends their hands over them, and an acclamation is sung as they leave the church with one of the catechists.

During the dismissal session, the Gospel of the day may be read one or more times as the catechumens and candidates reflect on its meaning in their lives. Once the liturgy has ended in church, the sponsors (and those spouses who wish to) join those already gathered for refreshments and an additional hour of catechesis. During this time, the catechist may share his or her own reflections on the readings of the day, the homily, and on some aspect of Christian teaching that may relate to the readings. The catechist often initiates a dialogue among the group, sometimes in small groups within the larger group.

Each year, as Lent draws near, those who have shown signs of a deeper conversion are invited into a discernment process that includes individual spiritual direction prior to the celebration of the rite of election.[45] Those who have discerned with their sponsors and the leadership of the parish initiation team a readiness to celebrate the sacraments of initiation at Easter gather for an overnight retreat with their sponsors, spouses, catechists, and the pastor. This retreat takes place on the grounds of the diocesan seminary the week before Lent begins. The rite of sending takes place at the Saturday evening liturgy for the vigil of the First Sunday of Lent, followed by a festive dinner. The following day, they gather once again for the rite of election, which takes place at the cathedral with the archbishop presiding.

A candidate for full communion might enter into the final discernment process at another time of the year and be received into the full communion of the Catholic Church at that time.

During Lent, those who will remain catechumens or candidates and those who have been called to the Easter sacraments continue to be dismissed from the Sunday Eucharist. Those who will celebrate the sacraments of initiation at Easter meet separately from those who will remain catechumens and candidates for both the dismissal and the catechetical session that follows. There they focus on their immediate preparation for the sacraments of initiation and reflect on the experience of the scrutinies that are celebrated on the Third, Fourth, and Fifth Sundays of Lent.[46]

The sacraments of initiation are celebrated at the Easter Vigil. Both baptisms and receptions of candidates into the full communion of the Catholic Church take place at this liturgy.[47] The director of initiation said that there were "no wimpy little symbols," only "big symbols" and "big gestures" at the Easter Vigil. Large quantities of fire, water, oil, bread, and wine allow the symbols to speak loud and clear about the importance of what is happening.

On Easter Wednesday, the whole parish is invited to the first session of mystagogy to reflect on the experience of the Easter Vigil. While most of the neophytes, those received into full communion, their sponsors, and catechists gather for this evening of reflection, only a small number of parishioners join in.

For the next full year, the neophyte and those received into full communion gather on the second Wednesday of each month to reflect on the Gospel and on how their experience of being Catholic Christians has changed them. They support and encourage one another in living out the faith in their daily lives. Mystagogy sessions often begin with a prayer experience that includes reading the Gospel from the previous Sunday and discussions similar to those held after the dismissals during the catechumenate.

The Interviews

The director described the initiation process "like a wheel. It's not a step up or a step down … at some point … you move on." She talked about the year-round process where inquirers can begin the process anytime during the year and move into the catechumenate whenever "they seem to be ready, [when] their questions change … [when there is] a deeper searching … [when] they realized that this is what they really want to do. [When] they're really committed to it." She noted that although it often took more than a year, "people are impressed that these people will take the time … to come into the church."

All of those I interviewed at St. John Chrysostom Parish had one thing in common. All of them were searching for something that they could not name. This theme of searching and finding was repeated over and over again in comments such as the following:

Anyone who comes here is certainly searching. Hopefully they've found a home.

I just really felt a need … a calling to come back to church.

I always felt that something was missing in my life. … It was something missing from me internally.

Something, I just felt, was unfinished or unresolved. … I feel finished now.

Something drew me here. I obviously wasn't getting it there [i.e., in another faith community]. I knew I was looking for more. I obviously couldn't find it on my own.

Over and over again, I heard statements about the importance of belonging to a community and of how each of the neophytes experienced this belonging. One of the neophytes expressed it this way:

One of the most significant [things], for myself, [is] the community here—just how very welcoming they are—very, very friendly. It is truly a parish that is very community based.

Others made statements such as these:

I saw the church, this church, as particularly warm and welcoming.

It's a family. It really is. ... It's such a loving and accepting society. ... It's a real tight-knit community. ... To finally be a part of that is very special.

They all spoke about their experience of the rite of acceptance into the order of catechumens as something significant:

The welcoming is great. It's wonderful. It was a little overwhelming for me.

I didn't think it would be that emotional. ... It was one of the real highlights.

The rite of welcoming was another [milestone]. ... We're outside the church, and the church comes out to meet us. That's an incredible experience.

The welcoming ... was an important step. Being part of the church is important to me.

However, this same neophyte also described the experience as "strange, because I had never seen it before."

They also spoke about their experiences of catechesis:

> I was pleasantly surprised that it wasn't rote teaching. ... I did need to explore what I felt and thought about God. I couldn't even say the word "God" or "Jesus" without feeling weird until I started the process. ... Discussing a religious story and the meanings behind it—there's a richness there you don't get unless you do that on a regular basis.

> They put Christ in a contemporary mind-set for us, to where we realized how he affects our daily lives. ... I could never put [the Scriptures] into perspective in my own life. ... In order to do that you have to get very close to the Bible. ... In order to understand the Scriptures, you need guidance. ... All the wonderful catechists we have here brought that into perspective for me.

The director of initiation called the dismissals "a sacred time." She described their experience as a "paradox," like the paradox of the cross. "They'll say that they really feel a part of the community" when they are dismissed from the Sunday assembly.

> [During the dismissal,] we would share our feelings, we would go over the homily. That would be explained to us, if we had any questions. Then we would reflect on something that we could relate personally to that.

> Every time we sit down ... and reflect on the reading, there's so much more there than you can get on a first time reading. I'm always amazed at the nuances of the stories, and the readings there were sort of revealed to me after somebody talked about it. It's always good to hear other people's reflections.

One neophyte looked back at the catechesis during the catechumenate and said the following:

I didn't think it was going to be as personalized as it was. I thought it was going to be a lot more stuffy than it was.

Another shared the following reflections:

The discussions of beliefs and teachings—that was more a strengthening of a faith I already had but was never nourished in any way. ... I [had] felt like I was kind of drifting without that formal training .... I had expected a little more nuts-and-bolts discussion about the traditions .... I think it's much more important to explore your feelings about God and strengthen that than to learn about the trappings of the church.

She also added this:

It was really important to have a sponsor, and I didn't realize what that would bring to the table exactly. ... I don't think they [i.e., the sponsors] realize how important it is just to get a taste of their depth of faith and some of that comfort level is kind of passed on.

Another neophyte said that she had "learned a tremendous amount from her" sponsor.

The weekend retreat before the celebration of the rite of election was a "highlight" for one of the catechumens. Another called it a "milestone." She also said this:

We [i.e., the catechumen, her fiancé, and her sponsor] were there for each other. ... That retreat just gave us a better insight into each other. ... It gave us the opportunity to do that.

In describing the Easter Vigil experience, the neophytes said the following:

It was a beautiful service. ... It was an awesome experience. ... We were all filled with incredible pride for the church. ... We had done a lot of soul searching, a lot of things about our values, our morals, what we wanted for the rest of our lives, what we wanted for our children and our spouses and the people important to us. We had done that for a year, some of us for more than a year. This was the culmination of a lot of hard work.

It was scary, definitely scary, to be there and to be going through all that, but then, in a sense it was and in a sense it wasn't. You just kind of forgot about the fear and got caught up in what was taking place.

It deserves something big and it was big. Very liberal with the oil. I really also enjoyed the first communion. It was nice to be part of the crowd. You just want to participate as fully as possible.

In discussing mystagogy, the director of initiation said this:

Our mystagogy sessions, some months we'll have almost everybody here and other months what we find is that most of the sponsors are here. The Scriptures have just meant so much to them that they don't want to lose that contact.

The neophytes, who were in the midst of mystagogy themselves, said the following:

It's nice to get back together and talk about the readings.

It's wonderful. You get to see everyone again—kind of touch base with everybody .... I'm very glad that we still do meet ... see each other ... talk about the homily and whatever else is going on.

It's good to see everybody. It's been really nice making that group of church friends. It's really important to see those people, to see what's going on in their lives. It's not just a surface interest in what these people are doing ... I kind of want to know how they're doing afterwards [i.e. after they have been initiated] ... seeing how it [i.e., their initiation] strengthened them.

Two of the neophytes talked about how their sons (both nine years old) had witnessed the changes in them and had asked if they, too, could join the initiation process. While I did not talk to the two boys,

their mothers described how they, too, had felt welcomed by the
community. Both were being raised by their mothers alone, and both
experienced a sense of both God's and the community's care for them.
One neophyte described her son this way:

He's probably changed more than I have. I think he's very, very
happy ... One of the things he's learned is to just pray about
[whatever bothers him] ... to deal with himself a little bit differently
... He really likes it here [at this parish], ... saying prayers at meals,
when he goes to bed.

She has also seen changes in herself and her behavior:

[I have] a whole different outlook ... spiritual, definitely, a more
spiritual outlook on things, just on life in general, just not to take
life so serious ... just leave it up to God's hands.

Several people I work with, they just can't quite figure it out,
what's really different, ... but they have actually said to me,
"What's going on here?"

My parents ... see a big change.

Another said this:

There have been a lot [of changes] in my life. [My husband] told my
sponsor, "She has really changed." I have been more at peace with
myself. It has affected the way I am with my husband and the kids
... I find myself being more patient with everybody. ... [At work,]
I'm questioning things more ... my values.

All of the neophytes also talked about their experience of the
Sunday Eucharist. They said things such as these:

I swear that every Sunday I go into church, that sermon has
something to do with what's going on in my life. Some way it puts
perspective into it. I know when I miss, and I really feel it. ... It
puts a calming effect on my whole life.

53

I don't think it's something you can come to once a week and then forget about it the rest of the week, and I don't. It just kind of rejuvenates your soul. ... I can't imagine not coming now. It most certainly makes a difference in the rest of my week.

When I go to Mass every week, it means something different to me. ... I experience it a little more deeply than someone who's been doing it all their life, only because I've been able to come to this point in my life as an adult, so I was aware of what I was doing. I was making choices on my own on this direction in my life.

I also find that coming to church on a regular basis is a very calming or restorative thing. ... I didn't realize that you kind of need religious exercise, like aerobics. If you don't do it, you're sort of out of shape, and coming to church every week is a nourishing thing. ... If you don't do it, you just don't feel right. ... I feel better on a weekly basis. I come here, dumb my problems, feel better and go home. I'm a better person. I'm more patient, a little kinder. It does really cause me to reflect on my relationships with people and what I've done during the week on a more regular basis.

All of the neophytes also said that it was important for them to get to know their pastor and the other priests and pastoral ministers on the parish staff. These relationships helped them know that their parish "stands behind you when you need them. It's amazing."

Two of the neophytes also talked about how the initiation experience has turned them into witnesses for their faith. They talked about how they talked to others about the importance of their faith. One said, "I share with other people about my experience here. ... I share my experience at least once a day."

This same neophyte ended my final interview at St. John Chrysostom Parish with this comment:

Every Sunday, when they [i.e., today's catechumens] get up and leave, I feel really glad for them. I feel very happy for them. And I know what they're going through isn't really easy, but I know they're in good hands. We really do pray for them, so they can follow that road. It's difficult. It never ends. It's a never-ending road, but you have certain milestones you'll never forget. That [i.e., the celebration of the sacraments of initiation] was one of them.

Chapter 2

Analysis of the Present Practices

The search for an effective mystagogy continues with an analysis of what the neophytes and mystagogues from St. Ambrose of Milan, St. Cyril of Jerusalem, and St. John Chrysostom Parishes described as their experience of the Christian initiation of adults, especially during the period of mystagogy.[1] The experiences shared by these neophytes and mystagogues show over and over again that the initiation process, and mystagogy in particular, can be effective. It can and does lead to behavioral changes in the lives of those who experience it. Thus, this chapter begins with a discussion of some of the ways in which the initiation process was effective.

The chapter will continue with a presentation of several common threads that emerged from an analysis of those interviews. It seems that an effective mystagogy recognizes that

1. inquirers come with several strong desires;

2. many people play significant roles in the initiation process; and

3. the process is focused on a life of faith.

My own experience with the Christian initiation of adults has, of course, colored my analysis. The neophytes and the stories of mystagogues I encountered in the four parishes and three diocesan training programs where I ministered have also influenced the analysis and the synthesis of the common threads I recognized in the stories shared during the interviews.

An Effective Mystagogy

One thing is certain from every interview I conducted—the initiation process has had both subtle and profound effects on the lives of those who have experienced it. Neophytes described how their lives had changed, how their attitudes had changed, and how their behaviors had changed. These changes not only included how the neophytes understood God, church, and faith but also included how they related to God, church, and other people.

Neophytes described how they treated members of their families, friends, acquaintances, and even strangers differently than they had previously. They talked about being more understanding, patient, and compassionate. They indicated that during the initiation process others often commented on how they had noticed positive changes in their behavior. Reconciliation occurred in several instances among family members who had been estranged for many years.

Neophytes who were parents indicated that their conversion had impacted not only their own lives but also the lives of their children. Frequently, relationships between parents and children grew closer, whether the children were adults, adolescents, or pre-adolescent children. In fact, in a number of cases, children old enough to choose for themselves saw changes in their parents and asked if they, too, could enter the initiation process. In each of these cases, parents and children seemed to grow even closer through the shared experience.

Several neophytes spoke about how their new faith had caused them to reevaluate their careers. In several cases, this led to changes in the way they treated employees, employers, or coworkers. In other cases, it led to career changes to somewhere the person felt he or she could be of more service to others. In one case, concern about justice in the workplace led a neophyte to establish his own company rather than continue to work for a corporation at which he felt that his previous management position forced him to act unjustly toward others.

It must be noted that some of these changes are rather recent, and therefore cannot be evaluated for their long-term effectiveness. However, in those few cases where I interviewed persons who were neophytes for several years, the effects seemed to endure. From the limited perspectives of the neophytes whom I interviewed, the whole initiation process was effective.

Inquirers Come with Several Strong Desires

Several neophytes expressed a conviction that something was missing from their lives before they found the parish in which they ultimately entered the initiation process and joined the church. These neophytes often did not know exactly what it was that was missing. They simply experienced a longing for something more in their lives. This was often described as an emptiness—an unfulfilled need. Some of them said that when they first came to their parish, they knew they had found what they were searching for, though they were often still unable to name what it was.

The Desire to Belong

More often than not, the neophytes I encountered talked about the experience of belonging. From the very beginning, they described their own desire to belong to something bigger than themselves. Many experienced a longing that led them to search for somewhere where they could belong. This desire to belong was often the first step in the initiation process. It preceded any sense of belonging to a particular community. It preceded any sense of belonging to God. It was this desire to belong that led to the search for community and for God.

Some neophytes described a feeling of belonging once they were fully initiated. Others experienced this belonging at the rite of election, when they were called by name and chosen for the Easter sacraments. Some experienced it at the rite of acceptance into the order of catechumens, particularly when the community gathered around them and prayed for them for the first time in a public way. Others said they felt like they belonged, as if they were "at home," from the very first moment they walked into their parish church for Sunday worship. Though the timing may have been different for each neophyte, all of them had some experience of belonging.

This feeling of belonging existed on multiple levels among the various neophytes interviewed. Some talked about belonging to God, to the people of God, or to the family of God. There was a sense that they belonged to something universal, something that transcends the limits of place and time. They also talked about belonging to a small community of faith made up of their fellow neophytes, sponsors, and catechists. This catechumenal community was very significant for many of the neophytes, who expressed a hope that somehow this community might continue to exist beyond the completion of the formal initiation process. The relationships involved in this group came to be treasured in the lives of many of the neophytes. Neophytes also talked about belonging to the parish community, the diocesan church, and the Roman Catholic Church. They viewed these particular belongings as significant for both the present and the future development of their faith.

This need to belong seems to be especially important in the dominant European-American culture of North America. The experience of belonging helps people overcome "the isolation which individuals feel and which the individualism of our culture makes us particularly prone to" (Schreiter, "Precious Blood Spirituality and CPPS Identity"). In many ways, this need to belong is as much a psychological need as it is a spiritual one. Some of the neophytes had tried to fulfill this need in other ways but found for themselves that it could only be satisfied in a relationship with God and God's people.

A Desire for the Eucharist

Almost all the neophytes talked about their experience of the Sunday Eucharist as both the beginning and the end of the initiation process. It was at the Sunday Eucharist when they first came to believe that their desire to belong could be fulfilled. It was at the Sunday Eucharist that they first encountered the parish as a community of faith. It was there that they first met priests whose preaching and presiding demonstrated a concern for the people of God. It was there that they first experienced a desire to share the Eucharist.

Likewise, most neophytes described being full participants in the Sunday Eucharist as one of the major goals of the initiation process. They often expressed a hunger for the Eucharist that grew stronger as the catechumenate approached its completion at the Easter Vigil. They spoke of how the Eucharist nourished them and helped them to face the week ahead and of how they looked forward to the weekly celebration.

Members of the parish initiation teams spoke of the importance of the Eucharist in their own lives and in the lives of the parish community. They described one of the primary goals of the initiation process as the continuing participation of neophytes in the Sunday Eucharist. They talked about how it was at the Eucharist that the parish came into being and was most profoundly itself. It was at the Eucharist that the church was church and where Christians were nourished and sent forth. The neophytes, in their conversations, confirmed that they, too, understood the Eucharist in this way.

Many People Play Significant Roles in the Initiation Process

The Community

The desire to belong is fulfilled in community. Over and over again neophytes and mystagogues described their parishes as communities. While the word has often been overused in our culture today to describe almost any group of people, the sense of community articulated by those I interviewed expressed a reality deeper than simply a group of people gathered together for a particular reason. Not every parish is a faith community, no matter how much we wish it were true.

A sense of community was often articulated as the reason a particular neophyte chose to join a particular parish. This sense of community was often experienced within the Sunday liturgy. Liturgy was often experienced as both worship of God and nourishment for God's people.

The descriptions offered by neophytes and mystagogues were verified in my own experience of the parishes. They rarely used the word *community*. There were no signs, announcements, or bulletin headings proclaiming, "We are a community." There was no need for them. There seemed to be a genuine sense of caring—a hospitality that was truly welcoming. While no one seemed to expect everyone to be a friend, a feeling of friendliness was expressed from the time I arrived until I left. I experienced this sense of community in conversations with staff and parishioners, in offices, meetings, and at the Sunday liturgy. I have not often had this experience in the parishes I have visited in my life.

This sense of community was not merely inwardly directed. In every parish I visited, I encountered a community that was outward looking as well. There were numerous opportunities to be of service to the larger community. The local community seemed to be a launching pad for ministry to those outside the community who were in need.

The Catechists

Neophyte after neophyte described the catechists in their parishes as women and men of faith—as storytellers who were not afraid to tell the story of their own spiritual lives. Neophytes told of how their catechists were willing to share stories of brokenness and healing, sinfulness and redemption. They talked about their catechists as women and men who knew God personally and intimately. Catechists did not just talk about God, they shared their experiences of God. They shared their own stories of God's mercy, compassion, and unbounded love.

In two of the parishes, the neophytes talked about "faith sharers." They told how these catechists, who had come to only one session during the process, had inspired them by their stories of faith. These people had no training or experience as teachers of faith. They simply witnessed how God had been at work in their own lives.

Neophytes were introduced to a living God by people who knew the joys and sorrows of life—who had experienced both the pain of the cross and the hope of the resurrection in their own lives—who believed that Jesus lives and walks with them through life.

Neophytes talked about catechists who believed in the real presence of God in the word proclaimed. Catechists, too, talked about how God continues to reveal Godself whenever the word is shared. This faith in the power of the word of God today seems to be significant for both neophytes and catechists.

It also seemed important, based on what the neophytes said, that some of the catechists have a background in Scripture, history, and doctrine. Their expertise enabled the neophytes to connect the

Scriptures, history, and doctrine of the church to their own lives of faith.

The Sponsors

The role of the sponsor seemed significant both when present and when absent. Most of the neophytes talked about how important it was for them to have a sponsor who walked with them through the initiation process and beyond. They spoke of the friendships that had developed and the encouragement they received from their sponsors. Many expressed sincere gratitude for the support they received and the relationship of care and concern for one another that developed along the way.

In all five parishes that I visited, a member of the initiation team assumed the responsibility of sponsor coordinator. This generally including recruiting and training of sponsors. Recruitment was often done through bulletin announcements, personal witness during the Sunday liturgy by someone who had been a sponsor in the past, and personal invitation by the sponsor coordinator. In most of the parishes, some combination of these three techniques was used. Training often involved one or more meetings of potential sponsors to discuss the responsibilities of the sponsor as described in the Rite (RCIA 10, et al.) and as understood by the sponsor coordinator. The entire initiation process was outlined, as well as the sponsor's role in the various rituals, catechetical sessions, and in the life of the candidate. Some of the parishes provided sponsors with additional reading materials, such as *The Guide for Sponsors* (Lewinski). The ministry of sponsor was described at every parish not as a teaching ministry but as one of accompaniment—the sponsor walks with the candidate without having to know all the answers to every question the candidate might have concerning faith or religion.

In those parishes in which the role of the sponsor was valued by the members of the parish initiation team, it was also experienced as significant by the neophytes. In these parishes, specific activities were often part of the catechetical sessions that involved personal dialogue between the candidates and their sponsors. In these parishes, the witness of the sponsor at the rite of sending was more than a mere formality. The sponsor not only publicly testified that the candidate was ready to proceed toward the celebration of the sacraments of initiation, he or she also played a significant role in the discernment process that preceded election. In these parishes, sponsors also continued to gather with those they sponsored during mystagogy and beyond.

In the one parish in which there was some doubt about the role of the sponsor in the minds of the initiation team members, close relationships between the sponsor and candidate did not regularly develop, formal structures for the sponsor to be part of the discernment prior to election did not exist, and sponsors rarely participated in any sessions during mystagogy. It was this same parish in which members of the initiation team wondered why so many neophytes stopped participating in the liturgical life of the parish within a short time after their initiation.

The Ordained Ministers

In all the parishes I studied, the pastors and other ordained ministers played significant roles in the initiation process. In addition to preaching and presiding at the various rites, the priests and deacons at these parishes participated in catechetical sessions and various discernment experiences. This included participation in retreats or days or evenings of prayer in preparation for the celebration of the various rituals. In each parish, the ordained ministers spent some time sharing their own stories of faith with inquirers and catechumens.

The neophytes experienced their pastors as concerned about their faith development. They talked about how they had come to know their pastors as persons. The personal involvement of the pastors in the entire initiation process was taken for granted by the neophytes. In my experience with training catechists in three dioceses, this is not considered the norm. In fact, catechists have often expressed frustration at the lack of participation in the Christian initiation of adults by the ordained members of the parish staff. Members of the parish initiation teams at the parishes I studied were aware that the personal involvement of the clergy in their parishes was rather unique, and they expressed a sense of appreciation for the support and encouragement this provided, not only for the candidates but also for themselves as ministers of the church.

The personal relationship between the neophytes and the clergy of the parish had a positive impact on the neophyte's experience of the rituals. When candidates knew those who preached and presided at the various rituals, they experienced the concern and support of the parish leadership as significant in their growing relationship to the church. Being known by name by those in positions of leadership seemed important to those who commented about their relationship to their pastors and pastoral associates.

Many of the catechists, as well as the neophytes, spoke about the clergy's preaching and presiding, both at the regular Sunday liturgy and at the special rituals of the Christian initiation of adults. They talked about homilies that related to their own lives and rituals, symbols, and gestures that were genuine and lavish. All of the pastors I observed at Sunday liturgy were relaxed, personable, and prayerful as they presided and preached. In conversation with them, all spoke about their concern for the faith development of all the people in their parish. The care with which they celebrated the Eucharist and shared the word of God with the people of God was a major contribution to the experience of belonging and the sense of community in these parishes.

The Process Is Focused on a Life of Faith

God Is Revealed in the Word

Catechists often talked about how they had originally thought that it was important to have a planned curriculum for the initiation process. They also described their own conversion to the belief that if they shared the word of God, following the lectionary cycle throughout the catechumenate and the period of purification and enlightenment, God would reveal to the catechumens (and candidates) all that was needed for them to become faithful members of the church.

Neophytes, too, expressed their own belief that God speaks to them in the Scripture readings each and every time they gather to celebrate the liturgy. They talked about how important it became, and often continues to be, to have the opportunity to reflect on the meaning of the readings in their own lives. Sometimes it was important to have some historical background, to know something more about the situation in which the passage was first proclaimed or the people involved in the story. However, this information was not just so they could understand the history better, but it was also so that they could understand what God was saying to them today.

Preachers and catechists who believe and witness to the living word of God seemed to enable neophytes to experience the real presence of God in the word in their own lives too.

The Goal of Initiation Is Living the Christian Life

In many parishes at which I spoke to members of the initiation team at workshops on the initiation process prior to this project, the goal of the Christian initiation of adults was often described as baptism. In almost every one of those parishes, few, if any, of the neophytes or their sponsors gathered for mystagogy sessions, and in a number of cases, neophytes stopped participating in the Sunday Eucharist before the first anniversary of their baptism.

In the parishes visited for this book, almost every team member I spoke to described the goal of initiation as living the Christian life, which includes, but is not limited to, participating in the Sunday Eucharist. It also includes a deep faith in God and a moral life that includes care for others, especially those in need.

In most cases, the neophytes I interviewed described the goal of initiation in the same terms as the catechists in their parishes. Several neophytes could not understand how someone could be baptized and not want to continue to learn about their faith or participate in the Eucharist on a weekly basis.

Passing On the Faith Is More Important Than Teaching Doctrine

Several of the mystagogues I interviewed had attended an Echoing God's Word Institute.[2] All of the mystagogues, at all five parishes visited, talked about using lectionary-based catechesis[3] during the catechumenate. They described the goal of catechesis as helping catechumens and candidates to develop a relationship with God and with the people of God.

Some neophytes said that they had originally expected that the catechetical sessions would be more like classes in which they would be taught church doctrine. They also said that they were pleased that the sessions were more focused on what they heard in the readings and the homily and how the word of God spoke to them. Sessions were more about their faith and how it affected their lives than on understanding church teachings.

Several neophytes mentioned that it was important for them to learn about church doctrine, and that they had learned how to do that and would continue to do so in the future. Even these catechumens said that though there are doctrines they still want to know more about, they were glad that the focus was more on their personal faith than on doctrine. They also mentioned that when they look back at their experience, they are surprised that they learned as much as they did.

Both the catechists and the neophytes talked about keeping that same focus on faith during mystagogy. A number of neophytes said they missed the conversations about the word of God that took place during the catechumenate and were glad that they still had the opportunity to do so occasionally during their first year as Roman Catholic Christians.

The Lavish Use of Symbols Communicates God's Grace

When describing the experience of the rituals, mystagogues and neophytes alike talked about the lavish use of symbols. Months, sometimes even years, later, communities gathered around candidates at the rite of acceptance, at grand celebrations of the rite of election in magnificent cathedrals, with large quantities of water flowing, splashing, and spilling all over the place, and copious amounts of oil were still remembered as signs of God's abundant blessings. When a thumbprint of oil on the forehead was deemed "enough" by those who planned or presided at anointings, those anointings were forgotten. When intercessions from the ritual book were used at the scrutinies, they, too, became lost memories. But when senses were signed with whole hands instead of fingers, when anointings were messy, when intercessions came from discussions that took place as part of the preparations for the celebrations, they were not only remembered, but they were remembered as experiences of the power of God at work in their lives today.

When symbols were lavish, the memory of the symbols itself was a spiritual experience. Neophytes who told of their ritual experiences often appeared to be reliving the experience in the telling of the story itself. Mystagogues and neophytes alike told of how others in the assembly experienced God at work when they watched rituals where powerful symbols spoke for themselves. They talked of being overwhelmed by emotion and by God's abundant graces as they were welcomed, anointed, chosen, scrutinized, baptized, confirmed, and led to the table.

Personal Discernment Is Essential to Faith Commitment

Mystagogues and neophytes alike talked about the importance of discernment in the initiation process. They talked about discernment in the context of spiritual direction or individual conversations with those in leadership in their parish initiation processes and in group processes in which catechumens and their sponsors spent time in prayer and reflection. They talked about retreat days, even weekends, where they had the opportunity to reflect on how God was calling them individually. They talked about how serious the decisions were when they prepared to move from one period to another.

Every neophyte who mentioned the discernment process mentioned how important it was to have the opportunity to seriously reflect on the steps they were taking and on where God was calling them. Many talked about how their relationship with their sponsor and with those in leadership in the parish grew closer as a result of some form of discernment process. This was especially significant in parishes where the clergy were involved in the discernment process.

Serious discernment was described as a necessary part of serious commitment. The one parish at which a number of neophytes did not attend mystagogy sessions and were no longer seen at the Sunday liturgy was also the one at which were there were few opportunities for discernment during the initiation process. This may indicate a correlation between discernment and committed membership.

Mystagogical Catechesis Begins with the Very First Rite

In each of the parishes I visited, mystagogical catechesis began with the celebration of the rite of acceptance into the order of catechumens. Sometime after the celebration, the new catechumens, their sponsors, and catechists gathered to reflect on the experience. The mystagogues asked questions such as these:

What did you see? Hear? Taste? Feel? Experience?

Where was God in this?

What did you learn about God? About Christ? About the church? About yourself from this experience?

By the time the neophytes gathered after Easter for the first time, these were not new questions. The process of remembering, reflecting, and discussing the experience of God in the rituals of the *Rite of Christian Initiation of Adults* was often described as a positive experience—even a necessary experience—especially by the time the celebration of the sacraments of initiation took place.

Some neophytes talked about asking themselves these questions when they returned home after the Sunday Eucharist. One neophyte even talked about doing this kind of remembering, reflecting, and discussing with her family around the dinner table each Sunday afternoon. They also expressed gratitude for the opportunities they had to gather during mystagogy to do this.

Some of the mystagogues talked about how they related the experiences of those who had taken part in the rituals with events from the Scriptures. They talked about Israel's passing through the Red Sea to freedom and the baptism of Jesus as similar experiences to those being described by the neophytes who had just been baptized.

As I asked neophytes to share their experience of Christian initiation with me, they often automatically moved to deeper questions of how they experienced God and what they learned about God, the church, and themselves through the process. Many of the neophytes seemed to be reliving the experience as they were telling it. Sometimes they would relate their own experience to an event described in Scripture. Often they would thank me at the end of our interview for providing them with the opportunity to remember once again the actions of God in their lives. Some commented on how they felt blessed to be able to tell the story one more time. I often felt blessed to have heard their stories too.

Some Conclusions

The testimony of the mystagogues and neophytes at St. Cyril, St. Ambrose, and St. John Chrysostom Parishes reveals thirteen major conclusions:

1. Christian initiation has behavioral effects on those who are initiated. These are especially evident in changing relationships that occur during and as a result of the process.

2. Inquirers often come with a strong desire to belong to something larger than themselves.

3. Inquirers often come with a strong desire to share the Eucharist, to be nourished in community by word and sacrament.

4. There is a strong sense of community in parishes that have an effective mystagogy.

5. Catechists are willing to share their own stories of faith as well as the history and the traditions of the church with inquirers, catechumens, and neophytes.

6. All involved in the process have a strong sense that God is revealed when the word of God is proclaimed and shared.

7. Passing on the faith is more important than teaching doctrine.

8. The lavish use of symbols in the liturgy communicates God's grace.

9. Personal discernment is essential for real faith commitment to occur.

10. Mystagogical catechesis (i.e., reflection on the experience of God in the rituals of the church) begins with the very first rite.

11. The goal of initiation is living the Christian life, not simply being baptized.

12. Sponsors witness their faith and offer concrete personal support to the catechumens and neophytes.

13. The clergy are personally involved in the catechesis and discernment as well as in the liturgical celebrations associated with the initiation process.

While many authors seem to have reached similar conclusions, the last three are rather unique to this study, and I would like to say more about them.

The Goal of Initiation Is Living the Christian Life

When the focus of the initiation process is baptism, the Easter Vigil can be experienced as a kind of graduation. The goal has been achieved. There is nothing else to do. This is especially evident when the initiation process is experienced as a part of marriage preparations or a way to strengthen familial relationships. If the goal is not focused on the life of faith, it can and often does end soon after baptism. Catechists, sponsors, priests, deacons, and other members of the community can often give the impression that baptism is the objective of the initiation process. Their words and deeds can give the false impression that baptism is the end of the road, rather than the beginning of the Christian life.

Many catechists and liturgists have described adolescent confirmation as "Graduation from Church." Once confirmed, most adolescents are rarely seen at the Sunday Eucharist or other parish activities. The same thing can, and I am afraid often does, happen when the Easter Vigil is the end of the initiation process, when the goal is baptism. I have often said to parents of seven-year-old children that I am not as concerned about their child's first communion as I am about their second, third, fiftieth, and one hundredth. The same might be said about Christian initiation. The focus ought not to be simply on baptism, confirmation, and first Eucharist. The goal of the initiation process ought to be on the next Eucharist, when one will be nourished again by word and sacrament to go forth and live the Christian life.

It seems clear to me that the initiation processes at St. Ambrose, St. Cyril, and St. John Chrysostom parishes were focused on living the Christian life and that it is precisely because of this focus that neophytes at these parishes continue to worship and participate in the faith life of the community.

Sponsors Witness Their Faith and Offer Concrete Personal Support

It seems rather significant that neophytes whose sponsors saw their role as ending with the celebration of the Easter Vigil were not around to be interviewed and, according to one sponsor who saw herself that way, no longer participated in the faith life of the parish community. It was likewise significant that all of the neophytes who were interviewed spoke about their ongoing relationship with their sponsor as an important part of their faith lives.

One of the primary ways in which the role of the sponsor was valued in the parishes that were part of this study was their role in discernment. They shared their own faith stories, listened to the faith stories of the catechumens they sponsored, testified to the community and to its leadership about the candidates. They also had developed relationships of friendship, which existed beyond the church and catechetical center walls. These relationships continued after the Easter Vigil and even beyond the experience of mystagogy.

Sponsors were viewed positively as sources of inspiration and motivation for the neophytes. The role did not end at the Easter Vigil or after the formal gatherings of mystagogy were complete. The relationships developed between sponsors and neophytes continued as the sponsors lived out their role as godparents. Traditionally, many have seen this as an important role for children, but it seems to be equally important for adults to have their godparents' support and encouragement as they continue to mature in their faith.

The Clergy Are Personally Involved in Catechesis and Discernment

The leadership of the clergy, especially pastors, also seems to be crucial to the effectiveness of the initiation process. They function in a role of leadership in the parish, and the neophytes experienced belonging and the care of the community, at least in part, through their priests and deacons. Their ability to preside and preach well was considered important, but just as significant was their willingness to share their own stories of faith, both within their homilies and in catechetical sessions.

Neophytes talked about knowing the clergy in the parish on a personal basis, which somehow allowed them to experience the liturgical leadership of their pastors in ways they did not experience in other parishes in which the presiders and preachers were strangers to them. The ordained ministers, who were willing to be vulnerable as they shared their own faith experiences, were also able to communicate the grace of God when they functioned in roles of liturgical leadership.

It is also significant, I believe, that each of the priests I had the opportunity to interview during my visits to St. Ambrose, St. Cyril, and St. John Chrysostom parishes shared their own experiences of conversion through their participation in the initiation process. Each of them expressed their conviction that God is at work in the rituals of the *Rite of Christian Initiation of Adults*. This faith in the process seems to correspond positively to the experience of those who participate in the process—neophyte, mystagogues, sponsors, and members of the assembly alike.

It seems to me that the best catechesis in the world will not make up for inadequate preaching and presiding. Good catechesis may make a difference in the short term, but for most Catholic Christians, the weekly experience of Eucharist, where the leadership of priests and deacons is so important, has more of an impact in the long run. Somehow, catechists, liturgists, and ordained ministers need to work together if the initiation process is to be effective over the long haul.

Chapter 3

The Church's Vision of Mystagogy

The search for an effective mystagogy continues with an examination of the church's vision of mystagogy. Two major sources will help us focus this vision. The first is the ancient tradition—especially during the late fourth century—as described by Hippolytus and Egeria and revealed in the preaching of four mystagogues: Cyril of Jerusalem, Ambrose of Milan, John Chrysostom, and Theodore of Mopsuestia.[1] The second is more contemporary—recent documents of the Roman Catholic Church, especially the *Rite of Christian Initiation of Adults*, which provides us with the Roman Catholic Church's official liturgical texts surrounding the initiation process for adults today. These two sources provide us with a historical and contemporary understanding of mystagogy. The one is based on a contemporary reading of the other. Those who wrote the *Rite of Christian Initiation of Adults* were greatly influenced by the initiation practices of the fourth century and used those practices as a model for developing a "catechumenate for adults, divided into several stages" which was "to be restored" according to instructions issued at Vatican II (CSL 64).

The Ancient Tradition

Hippolytus[2] (✦ c. 235): *The Apostolic Tradition*

The fourth-century mystagogues followed a baptismal practice related, at least in part, to the process described in the *Apostolic Tradition* (Cuming, especially 16–24).[3] This ancient document, often attributed to Hippolytus,[4] describes what some in church believed

75

should be the practices for the whole church. This insistence may indicate that these were, in fact, not the general practices of the church at the time of his writing, but were the practices followed in Rome with the hope that they would be adopted elsewhere. Hippolytus described numerous liturgical practices; among them are some rituals related to the initiation of adults. What follows is a brief outline of those practices.

The initiation process is described for adults, but the text also instructs the following, indicating that infants, too, were baptized at this time in the church at Rome:

> Baptize the little ones first. All those who can speak for themselves shall do so. As for those who cannot speak for themselves, their parents or someone from their family shall speak for them (AT 21).

The first step in the process is admission as hearers of the word, also called catechumens. In order to be admitted to the word, one was first "brought to the teachers before all the people arrive" and was to "be questioned about their reason for coming to the faith" (AT 15). This examination included questions about social status, that is, married or single; free, master, or slave; and profession or trade. Once a person becomes a hearer, Hippolytus says this:

> Catechumens shall continue to hear the word for three years. But if [someone] is keen, and perseveres well in the matter, the time shall not be judged, but only [the person's] conduct (AT 17).

Therefore, it seems likely that many people spent less than a full three years as catechumens. Apparently, the catechumens listened to the word with the believers, were instructed by a teacher, and then would "pray by themselves, separated from the faithful" (AT 18). "After their prayer, when the teacher [had] laid hands on the catechumens, he [would] pray and dismiss them" (AT 19). This was the practice, whether the teacher was a cleric or layperson.

After this time as catechumens, a second examination would take place:

> And when those who are to receive baptism are chosen, let their life
> be examined; have they lived good lives when they were
> catechumens? Have they honoured the widows? Have they visited
> the sick? Have they done every kind of good work? And when
> those who have brought them bear witness to each ..., let them
> hear the Gospel (AT 20).

This indicates that the focus of initiation for catechumens, prior to
being chosen for baptism, was the hearing of the Hebrew Scriptures
and the letters of the apostles. They did not hear the Gospel until they
were "chosen" for baptism. Once chosen, they not only heard the
Gospel, but hands were "laid on them daily while they [were]
exorcised" (AT 20). On the Friday and Saturday before baptism, the
catechumens were instructed to fast, and more intense exorcisms took
place with the bishop presiding and the chosen ones kneeling in
prayer. In addition to the laying on of hands, the bishop also
"breathe[d] on their faces, and when he had signed their foreheads,
ears and noses, he ... raise[d] them up" (AT 20).

That Saturday evening, a prayer was said over the water and the
chosen ones removed their clothing and declared, "I renounce you,
Satan, and all your service and all your works" (AT 21). Then they
were anointed with the oil of exorcism, which the bishop had just
blessed. The person entered the font with a deacon and was then
baptized three times while answering the following questions:

> [Do you] believe in one God, the Father almighty?
>
> Do you believe in Christ Jesus, the Son of God, who was born of the
> holy Spirit from the Virgin Mary, and was crucified under Pontius
> Pilate, and died, and rose again on the third day alive from the
> dead, and ascended into heaven, and sits at the right hand of the
> Father and will come to judge the living and the dead?
>
> Do you believe in the holy Spirit, and the holy church, and the
> resurrection of the flesh? (AT 21).

Upon coming out of the water, the neophyte was anointed by a
presbyter with the oil of thanksgiving, which was also blessed by the

bishop just prior to baptism. The neophyte was then brought into the church, where the bishop then laid hands on the newly baptized, prayed for them, and anointed them again with the oil of thanksgiving. The bread and wine mixed with water were offered, as were milk and honey. "And the bishop [gave] a reason for all these things to those who receive[d]" (AT 21).

After baptism, Hippolytus instructed his readers:

> We have handed over to you in brief these things about holy baptism and the holy offering, for you have already been instructed about the resurrection of the flesh and the other things as it is written, But if there is anything else which ought to be said, the bishop shall say it privately to those who have received baptism. Unbelievers must not get to know it, unless they first receive baptism (AT 21).

The revelation that there are some things that the bishop should tell "privately to those who have received baptism" is the first textual suggestion that some form of mystagogy existed in the early third century. Though Hippolytus told us about various persons, about baptismal practices, the Eucharist, orders, prayers, blessings, and other practices of the early church, he was not at all clear about what the "anything else which ought to be said" might be. This instruction, however, does suggest that some kind of postbaptismal catechesis did take place, and that the bishop had a significant role in imparting it to the neophytes.

By the end of the fourth and the early fifth centuries, we have the actual texts of some of these mystagogical instructions. These homilies provide us with an image of what the initiation process looked like at that time and a vision of mystagogy, which, at least in part, inspired its rebirth after Vatican II.

The Preaching of Cyril of Jerusalem (✦ c. 386/7)

Cyril was bishop of Jerusalem from about 350 to 386/7.[5] Among his writings are a series of instructions he gave to those preparing for baptism, whom he called "those to be enlightened" or "those being enlightened" (McCauley vol.1, 1). These instructions, called the

Catecheses, were delivered during Lent, as explanations of the Jerusalem Creed.[6] The existing texts were probably notes taken by listeners during his preaching in 348/9,[7] while he was still a presbyter. Several of the *Catecheses* may be from his preaching from later years as well.

These sermons might be described as exhortations to the Elect as they prepare for the celebration of initiation at the vigil of Easter. They not only imparted information about and explanations of the Creed, but also were aimed at conversion of mind and heart. Prior to baptism, those being enlightened were encouraged to change their lives, to turn away from sinful thoughts and behaviors, and to live as faithful disciples of the Lord.

After becoming a bishop around 350, Cyril preached the *Mystagogic Catecheses* to those who had recently been baptized.[8] These instructions were given during Easter week. They describe what happened during the various rites that were part of the vigil of Easter, with an emphasis on encouraging the neophytes to live out the reality of what had happened in them because of these rites. The rituals of baptism, anointing, and Eucharist had never been witnessed or explained to the neophytes prior to their experience. The mystagogical exhortations were to enliven the faith planted by God in the hearts of those who had just experienced the mysteries (i.e., the sacraments of initiation) for the first time.

Both the *Catecheses* and the *Mystagogic Catecheses* were preached every year.[9] Believers often joined those being enlightened or the neophytes in order to reinvigorate their faith and offer support to those who were coming to or just experienced the mysteries for the first time.

Cyril's mystagogy lasted but one week, during which the neophytes and any interested believers gathered for daily prayer and instruction. Cyril basically led those gathered through a remembering of what had happened during the vigil of Easter and explained each of the ritual elements. He expressed the reason for this when he said:

> These daily instructions on the mysteries, and these new teachings which proclaim new tidings, are useful to us all, but especially to you who have been granted new life from old age to rebirth. Therefore I must describe to you the stage which follows ..., so that

you may know what was underlying the symbolic acts you performed. ... (MC 2, 1).[10]

On the following day, he gave them similar advice:

Now that you have been "baptized into Christ" and have "put on Christ," you have become conformed to the Son of God. ... Hence, since you "share in Christ," it is right to call you Christs or anointed ones. ... All the rites carried out over you have a symbolic meaning (MC 3, 1).

The rituals of the Easter vigil are the foundations on which mystagogical preaching is built. The symbolic acts were experienced first, and only then, according to Cyril, could their underlying or symbolic meaning be shared.

Each of Cyril's mystagogical instructions is preceded by a reading from one of the apostolic letters.[11] He frequently used events and images from the Scriptures to relate recent experiences to the history of God's saving deeds. Events from the Hebrew Scriptures were related to events in the life of Jesus and in the lives of the neophytes and believers.

Here the style of patristic exegesis is clearly at work; that is, a scriptural explanation which sees the important persons, events and objects of the New Testament foreshadowed by other people, events or objects in the Old Testament—the baptized, immersed in the waters of baptism are saved from the fierce enemy as the Israelites were saved from Pharaoh by the waters of the Red Sea (Regan 16).

Cyril's preaching indicates that the bishop was actively involved in the initiation process, meeting with the catechumens and neophytes on many occasions. This was especially true during Lent and the postbaptismal mystagogy of Easter week, when he met with them almost daily, sharing his insights with those about to be or just having been initiated into the church.

There seems to be a strong conviction in Cyril's preaching that God is at work both in the Scriptures and in the celebrations of the mysteries. There is also a strong call to respond to the gifts received by living lives of faithful service to God and to those in need. Faith has practical and behavioral consequences for those who have experienced the grace of God. Cyril's preaching calls forth a sense of wonder at what God has done and a sense of responsibility to live up to the grace received.

The Witness of Egeria (c. 381–384)

A woman, known today as Egeria,[12] traveled to Jerusalem between 381 and 384,[13] where she may have actually heard the preaching of Cyril. Throughout her travels, she sent descriptions of what she saw, heard, and experienced back to her "loving sisters" in Gaul or Spain (Wilkinson 24.1 et al.; 3). Her descriptions give us an outline of the initiation process as celebrated in Jerusalem at that time.

Throughout the year, believers and catechumens gathered several times a day for prayer at the Anastasis, believed to have been Christ's tomb, where they prayed, sang psalms, listened to Scripture readings and preachings. Egeria wrote this:

> After a prayer the catechumens are blessed, then the faithful, and they have the dismissal (ET 34).[14]

They often gathered at the cross[15] immediately following these times, and the separate blessings for both the catechumens and the believers were offered once again.

The day before Lent begins, those who were to be baptized gave their names to one of the priests. On the first day of Lent, the catechumens who presented themselves stood before the bishop and the community with their godparents.

> Then one by one those seeking baptism are brought up, men coming with their [god]fathers and women with their [god]mothers. As they come in one by one, the bishop asks their neighbours questions about them: "Is this person leading a good life? Does he respect his parents? Is he a drunkard or a boaster?" He asks about all the serious human vices. And if his inquiries show him that someone has not committed any of these misdeeds, he himself puts

81

down his name; but if someone is guilty he is told to go away, and
the bishop tells him that he is to amend his ways before he may
come to the font. He asks the men and the women the same
questions (ET 45.2–45.4).

In Jerusalem, at the time, Lent lasted eight weeks. Many people
fasted five days a week, from Monday through Friday (ET 27.1). In this
way, there were forty days of fasting during Lent, and on each day of
fast, those who were to be baptized were "exorcised by the clergy first
thing in the morning" (ET 46.1). Likewise,

> As soon as that has taken place, the bishop's chair is placed in the
> Great Church, the Martyrium, and all those to be baptized, the men
> and the women, sit round him in a circle. There is a place where the
> [god]fathers and [god]mothers stand, and any of the people who
> want to listen (the faithful, of course) can come in and sit down,
> though no catechumens, who do not come in while the bishop is
> teaching (ET 46.1).

> His subject is God's Law; during the forty days he goes through the
> whole Bible, beginning with Genesis, and first relating the literal
> meaning of each passage, then interpreting its spiritual meaning.
> He also teaches them at this time all about the resurrection and the
> faith. And this is called catechesis. After five weeks' teaching they
> receive the Creed, whose content he explains article by article in the
> same way as he explained the Scriptures, first literally and then
> spiritually. Thus all the people in these parts are able to follow the
> Scriptures when they are read in church, since there has been
> teaching on all the Scriptures from six to nine in the morning all
> through Lent, three hours' catechesis a day (ET 46.2).

During Holy Week, which was called the Great Week (ET 30.1) in
Jerusalem at the time, each of the catechumens whose names had
been inscribed on the first day of Lent stood before the bishop with his
or her godparent and recited the Creed. During the homily that
followed, Egeria reported that the bishops said the following:

"During these seven weeks you have received instruction in the
whole biblical Law. You have heard about the faith, and the
resurrection of the body. You have also learned all you can as
catechumens of the content of the Creed. But the teaching about
baptism itself is a deeper mystery, and you have not the right to
hear it while you remain catechumens. Do not think it will never be
explained; you will hear it all during the eight days of Easter after
you have been baptized. But so long as you are catechumens you
cannot be told God's deep mysteries" (ET 46.6).

Egeria stated that "they keep their paschal vigil like us ..."
(ET 38.1). Because we do not know how the vigil was observed at her
home, we have few details about how it was celebrated in Jerusalem.
She did, however, tell us this:

As soon as the "infants"[16] have been baptized and clothed, and left
the font, they are led with the bishop straight to the Anastasis. The
bishop goes inside the screen and after one hymn, says a prayer for
them. Then he returns with them to the church, where the people
are keeping vigil in the usual way (ET 38.1ff.).

This ritual was, of course, unique to Jerusalem. Immediately after
baptism, the neophytes visited the empty tomb—not a representation
of the empty tomb, but what was actually believed to have been the
empty tomb of Jesus the Christ.

Mystagogy was only one week long, but it was, according to
Egeria, a week filled with excitement. The whole community
worshiped together at the holy sights in Jerusalem, at Gethsemane and
Golgotha, at the empty tomb and mountain of the ascension, and at
Mount Zion. The neophytes were blessed at each of these sacred
places and shared in the liturgies of Easter week.

Once each day of Easter week after morning prayer,

the bishop stands leaning against the inner screen in the cave of
the Anastasis, and interprets all that takes place in Baptism. The
newly baptized come into the Anastasis, and any of the faithful
who wish to hear the Mysteries; but while the bishop is teaching,
no catechumen comes in, and the doors are kept shut in case any

try to enter. The bishop relates what has been done, and interprets it, and, as he does so, the applause is so loud that it can be heard outside the church. Indeed the way he expounds the mysteries and interprets them cannot fail to move his hearers (ET 47.2).

To hear the explanations of the mysteries while gathered at what was to believed to have been the tomb of Christ must have influenced the way in which mystagogy was experienced.

Egeria's witness as a visitor in Jerusalem for the first time confirms that mystagogy is a time of great excitement as the neophytes celebrate their new life in Christ and discover the secret meaning of the baptism they have received. Like those who had just experienced the mysteries of baptism and Eucharist, Egeria was filled with awe at the wonder of God's grace revealed in these sacred rites.

The Preaching of Ambrose of Milan (✦ 397)

Ambrose was elected bishop of Milan while still a catechumen in 373. His sermons *On the Sacraments* to the newly baptized were preached during Easter week, probably sometime between 380 and 391.[17] These six sermons were later edited by Ambrose as *On the Mysteries*.[18]

Ambrose began his series of postbaptismal sermons, much as Cyril did, by explaining that he could not tell them everything about the sacraments until after they had received them:[19]

I shall begin now to speak of the sacraments which you have received. It was not proper for me to do so before this, because, for the Christian, faith must come first. That is why, at Rome, the baptized are called the faithful; and our father Abraham was made just not by his works but by faith. So you were baptized and came to believe. It would be impious for me to conclude otherwise. You would never have been called to grace, had not Christ judged you worthy of grace (OS 1, 1).[20]

For Ambrose, faith comes from God through the experience of the sacraments. Understanding can only come after faith. One cannot possibly understand until one has experienced the sacrament.

Ambrose believed that explaining the sacrament prior to its experience would be useless. The explanation of the sacraments is not withheld until after they are experienced because it is a secret to be kept from the uninitiated, but because Ambrose believed one could never understand their meaning until after the experience.[21]

On the first three days of the week after Easter, Ambrose focused on the experience of baptism, and on the last three days, he primarily spoke about the Eucharist. In describing the various ritual elements experienced by the neophytes at the Easter Vigil, Ambrose told us something about the liturgical practices at Milan at that time. The rite began with the "mysteries of the Opening" (OS 1, 2–3) the Ephphetha, when the bishop touches the ears and nostrils of the those about to be baptized.[22] Another ritual not found in Rome at the time of Hippolytus or Jerusalem at the time of Cyril or Egeria was the washing of the feet, which Ambrose defended against those in Rome for whom it was not a custom (OS 3, 4–7).

Like Cyril of Jerusalem, he reminded the neophytes of their experience and then shared with them its meaning. He, too, related the various words and actions of the sacraments of initiation to the Scriptures.

> The most striking thing about them [i.e., the mystagogical sermons] is the bold use that Ambrose makes of the allegorical method of interpreting the Scriptures. ... The presupposition of this exegetical method is that, as all truth comes from the Holy Spirit, the words of Scripture can be used to illuminate any truth to which they can be made to apply (Yarnold 98–99).

For Ambrose, the sacraments and the Scriptures were mirrors of a far greater reality, an archetype found in heaven. It is that spiritual reality that is of most importance for the life of the believer. That reality is revealed in the events found in both the Hebrew and Christian Scriptures and in the sacramental events experienced by Christians today. These events are essentially related to one another because they are related to the same spiritual reality.

The peculiarity of the typological method consists precisely in this, that through the parallelism of events it brings to light the unity of the divine plan. ... Typology unites past, present and future.[23]

Mystagogy connects the recent experiences of the neophytes with the actions of God in the Hebrew Scriptures, in the Christian Scriptures, and in the spiritual realm where God dwells. It proclaims the power of God at work throughout history. Ambrose said the following:

The Lord commanded and the heavens were made, the Lord commanded and the earth was made, the Lord commanded and the seas were made, the Lord commanded and all creatures came into being. See, then, how efficacious the word of Christ is. If then, there is such power in the word of the Lord Jesus that things begin to exist which did not exist before, how much more powerful it is for changing what already existed into something else (OS 4, 15).

This same logic was used to explain how bread and wine are changed into the body and blood of Christ and how the neophytes became "new creations" in Christ. The power of God's word is a central aspect of Ambrose's theology, and his mystagogy proclaims that message over and over again. The mystagogical sermons of Ambrose, thus, are meant to inspire the neophytes to recognize God's actions in their own lives, actions that are prefigured in the Hebrew Scriptures, revealed in Christ, and ritualized in the sacraments.

The Preaching of John Chrysostom (✦ 407)

Before becoming bishop of Constantinople in 397, John Chrysostom preached several series of mystagogical instructions. There are three manuscripts that represent at least three different sets of mystagogical preaching by John Chrysostom. One complete series of eight instructions exists and is thought to have been preached in Antioch around 390. It is this complete series we shall examine in our search for an effective mystagogy (Mazza 108–109).

John Chrysostom gave two sermons about baptism prior to its celebration at Easter. Then he gave six sermons during Easter week concerning the consequences of baptism. His first instruction, "addressed to those about to be baptized" (BI 1, 1),[24] begins like this:

> This is a time of joy and gladness of the spirit. Behold, the days of our longs and love, the days of your spiritual marriage, are close at hand. ...
> Truly today there is joy in heaven and on earth. ...
> Come, then, let me talk to you as I would speak to a bride about to be led into the holy nuptial chamber. Let me give you, too, a glimpse of the Bridegroom's exceeding wealth and of the ineffable kindness which He shows to His bride (BI 1, 1–3).

John Chrysostom sought to encourage, to excite his listeners, and to relate their experience of baptism to everyday experiences that his listeners might understand. His mystagogical preaching was "concerned with stirring the emotions and giving moral instruction. ... [He] makes much of the awe which the sacraments should inspire" (Yarnold 151). "His mystagogy stresses elements not present like anything to the same extent in the mystagogy of the other Fathers of the Church: the continual emphasis on Christian moral behavior" (Mazza 109). The mysteries of baptism and Eucharist have consequences. They call for, they demand, a response, and that response is a life worthy of the name Christian.

> Henceforth, through the kindness of God, you will be called a Christian and one of the faithful. ... Soon you will put on Christ. You must act and deliberate in all things with the knowledge that He is everywhere with you (BI 1, 44).

> In view of the great honor He bestows, you should dispose your hearts well and be willing to contribute your fair share. If you do so, how generous a recompense do you think the loving God will deem that you deserve? (BI 2, 1).

Unlike Cyril and Ambrose, John Chrysostom did not discuss the actual rituals of baptism and Eucharist with the neophytes. While he made occasional references to elements of the baptismal ritual, there was no systematic explanation of Eucharist at all in his instructions.

His focus was on future behavior and future blessings. His final words to the neophytes demonstrated this eschatological focus:

> And especially, I do exhort you who have recently put on Christ and received the descent of the Spirit. Each day look to the luster of your garment, that it may never receive any spot or wrinkle, either by untimely words, or idle listening, or by evil thoughts, or by eyes which rush foolishly and without reason to see whatever goes on. Let us build a rampart about ourselves on every side and keep constantly before our minds that dread day, so that we may abide in our shining brightness, keep our garments of immortality unspotted and unstained, and deserve those ineffable gifts. May it come to pass that we all obtain those gifts by the grace and loving-kindness of our Lord Jesus Christ (BI 8, 25).

This passage likewise demonstrates John Chrysostom's frequent use of metaphor, used here in reference to the white garments, but he also used metaphors throughout his preaching to connect the various ritual elements of the sacraments to the moral life of the Christian.

John Chrysostom followed the tradition of the other mystagogues, making constant use of typology as he related Scripture passages to the sacrament of baptism and to the lives of the neophytes. In his third instruction, he said, "Learn the power of the type, that you may learn the strength of the truth" (BI 3, 13). His use of typology, however, often related past events to future behavior and to the rewards of salvation that can only be experienced at the end of time.

The Preaching of Theodore of Mopsuestia (✦ 427)

Before becoming bishop of Mopsuestia in 392, Theodore, like John Chrysostom, had served as a presbyter in Antioch. He and John Chrysostom knew each other and preached their catechetical and mystagogical sermons within a few years of each other.[25] The teachings of Theodore were condemned in the sixth century, and almost all of his writings destroyed.[26] However, there exists today Syriac translations of seventeen homilies that are often divided into two series. The first ten deal with the Creed and are believed to have been preached during Lent as part of the preparation for baptism

(Mingana vol. 5). The remaining seven consist of one on the Lord's Prayer, three on baptism, and two on the Eucharist (Mingana vol. 6). These homilies are often considered mystagogical.[27] This division into two sets of homilies is based on notes by the Syriac translator at the end of the tenth[28] and beginning of the eleventh homilies. These homilies were probably preached at Antioch between 383 and 392. In the first of the homilies, Theodore said the following:

Those who are about to partake now of these awe-inspiring mysteries are inspired to do so by the grace of God. They do not do this in order to partake of small and ordinary gifts, but to be transformed completely into new men [and women] and to possess different virtues which they will receive by the gift of the grace of God: being mortal they will become immortal, being corruptible they will become incorruptible, ... being changeable they will become unchangeable, being bond [i.e., slaves] they will become free, being enemies they will become friends, being strangers they will become sons [and daughters] (BH 5, 20).[29]

Passages like these are meant to encourage and inspire those whose names have been inscribed for baptism as they prepare for the great feast of Easter. What follows in the prebaptismal catechesis are a series of explanations of the Creed. Theodore explains why he is doing this when he said this:

Now which is the faith and which are the promises through which we have our part in mysteries in the hope of these heavenly gifts in which we will delight? These are found in the profession of faith which we make before Christ our Lord at the time of our baptism. If it were possible to comprehend their power by hearing only, our words would have been useless, because their mere recitation would have made them understood by those who heard them. Since, however, there is much power hidden in them—as our holy Fathers confided to us from the gift of God an ineffable treasure condensed in words which are easy to learn and to remember—it is necessary to teach those who are about to receive these mysteries and to show them the sense and the meaning that are hidden in them. When they have learnt the greatness of the gift to which they wish to make their approach, and have understood the meaning of their religion and their promises for the sake of which they receive such a great gift, they will keep with diligence in their souls the faith which has been handed down to them (BH 5, 21).

The same motivation seemed to guide Theodore in his mystagogical preaching. He sought to encourage and inspire his listeners to live the new life they had received in baptism and the Eucharist. He likewise sought to reveal to the neophytes all that is hidden in the baptismal and eucharistic rituals. Like John Chrysostom, Theodore explained the meaning of baptism before it was celebrated, giving his listeners the following reasons for doing so:

> As, however, the time of the sacrament has drawn near, and you are by the grace of God about to participate in holy baptism, it is right and necessary that we should explain before you the power of the sacrament and of the things which are accomplished in it, and the reason for which each of them is accomplished, in order that when you have learnt what is the reason for all of them you may receive the things that take place with great love.
>
> Every sacrament consists in the representation of unseen and unspeakable things through signs and emblems. Such things require explanation and interpretation, for the sake of the person who draws nigh until the sacrament so that he [or she] might know its power. If it only consisted of the (visible) elements themselves, words would have been useless, as sight itself would have been able to show us one by one all the happenings that take place, but since a sacrament contains the signs of things that take place or have already taken place, words are needed to explain the power of signs and mysteries (BH 6, 17).

We sacramentally perform the events that took place in connection with Christ our Lord, in order that—as we have learnt from experience—our communion with Him may strengthen our hope. It would be useful, therefore, to discuss before you the reason for all the mysteries and signs (BH 6, 21).

Theodore went into great detail about the baptismal ritual that was about to be experienced, giving three lengthy discourses on baptism prior to its celebration. Like the other mystagogues, Theodore used events from their everyday experiences, as well as events from the Hebrew and Christian Scriptures, to help them understand the great mysteries they were about to celebrate. He used allegory and typology to relate the experience the people of God throughout history to the reality that they would experience in the sacraments.

Theodore waited until after baptism, until "an opportune time" (BH 6, 70–71), to discuss the sacrament of Eucharist. These final two homilies are the only two preached during Easter week. Though the homilies on baptism are mystagogical in nature, one needs to recall that they were not preached during what the Rite today considers the period of mystagogy but rather during the final days prior to the celebration of Easter.

> The purpose of mystagogy for Theodore is to instill an understanding of the power and the purpose of the mystery, whether this be taken globally or in the individual units of ritual that make it up. By its nature, the mystery tends to lead the participating faithful to salvation. It follows that the knowledge of the mystery at its deepest level must lead the faithful to so intense and lively a participation that the mystery is enabled to achieve its ultimate purpose: the communication of salvation (Mazza 54–55).

Theodore not only used typology but also moved into allegory, especially in his preaching on the Eucharist, in which almost every action is somehow related to the sacrifice of Christ on the cross. The earthly liturgy is an allegorical representation of both what Christ has already done and of the heavenly liturgy in which we shall one day participate.

Some Conclusions

Several common threads can be discovered in the teachings of Hippolytus, the witness of Egeria, and the preaching of Cyril, Ambrose, John Chrysostom, and Theodore. They all seem to demonstrate that they held some common principles out of which their practices arose. These include the following:

1. The Creed, the Lord's Prayer, and the mysteries (i.e., the sacraments of initiation) are primary vehicles for God's revelation.

2. There are divine realities that we can and do experience in symbolic form and that can be understood through the use of typology or allegory.

3. The Scriptures, too, have a deeper meaning that helps to reveal these same divine realities that were foreshadowed in the events of the Hebrew Scriptures, fulfilled in the events of the Christian Scriptures, symbolically experienced in the rituals of the church, and that we will one day experience in heaven.

4. The bishop and clergy have a special responsibility to help the believers understand these deeper realities through their preaching.

5. The sponsors/godparents have a major responsibility to witness to the community about the worthiness or readiness of the catechumens to partake in the mysteries.

6. There are behavioral consequences to the faith—a moral life is the only adequate response to God's salvation.

7. Initiation leads to participation in the Eucharist, where God most clearly reveals the salvation Christ has gained for all believers.

8. There are some aspects of the faith—of one's relationship with God—that one can only enter into, appreciate, or understand after having experienced the mysteries. For some of the late-fourth-century mystagogues, this includes the deeper meanings of baptism. For all of them, it includes the divine realities revealed in the Eucharist.

9. The catechesis of Lent, explaining the Creed and Lord's Prayer, are intimately related to the mystagogy of (Lent and) Easter, explaining the mysteries.

10. All of the catechesis takes place within a liturgical context, where catechumens (during Lent) and neophytes (during Easter week) gather with other believers for prayer, Scripture readings, and reflection.

These principles give us a glimpse of the church's vision of mystagogy in the late fourth century.

A Contemporary Vision

We now jump more than fifteen hundred years to look at a contemporary vision of mystagogy.[30] This vision is primarily expressed in several documents of the Roman Catholic Church:

- documents of Vatican II, especially:

  - *The Constitution on the Sacred Liturgy*
  - *The Decree on the Pastoral Office of Bishops in the Church*
  - *The Decree on the Church's Missionary Activity*

- post-conciliar documents:

  - *Rite of Christian Initiation of Adults: The Provisional Text (1974)* and *The Complete Text with American Additions (1988)*
  - *The Code of Canon Law*
  - *Catechism of the Catholic Church*

The rest of this chapter will consist of a survey of these sources for developing a contemporary vision of mystagogy.

Vatican II: An Invitation to Rediscover the Catechumenate

The Second Vatican Council's first decree, approved at the end of its first session, December 1963, was the *Constitution on the Sacred Liturgy*.[31] This document set the stage for all that would follow. Its opening words seek to explain the reason for the Council's reforms, not just the liturgical reforms, but all that would be accomplished as a result of the Council:

> The Sacred Council has several aims in view: it desires to impart an ever increasing vigor to the Christian life of the faithful; to adapt more suitably to the needs of our own times those institutions that are subject to change; to foster whatever can promote union among all who believe in Christ; [and] to strengthen whatever can help to call the whole of humanity into the household of the Church. The Council therefore sees particularly cogent reasons for undertaking the reform and promotion of the liturgy (CSL 1).

Among the decisions of the Council Fathers related to this reform was the reestablishment of the catechumenate. This is what they wrote:

> The catechumenate for adults, divided into several stages, is to be restored and put into use at the discretion of the local Ordinary. By this means the time of the catechumenate, which is intended as a period of well-suited instruction, may be sanctified by sacred rites to be celebrated at successive intervals of time (CSL 64).

> Both of the rites of baptism for adults are to be revised: not only the simpler rite, but also the more solemn one, with proper attention to the restored catechumenate (CSL 66).

Two years later, the Council issued the *Decree on the Church's Missionary Activity*.[32] They had spent some more time reflecting on the initiation process. After the initial comments concerning the restoration of the catechumenate in *Constitution on the Sacred Liturgy*, the Council Fathers had more to say about their reasons for reestablishing the catechumenate:

Under the movement of divine grace, the new convert sets out on a spiritual journey by means of which, while already sharing through faith in the mystery of the death and resurrection, he passes from the old person to the new who has been made perfect in Christ. This transition, which involves a progressive change of outlook and morals, should be manifested in its social implications and effected gradually during the period of catechumenate (DCMA 13).

They likewise had more to say about the structure of the catechumenate and the adult initiation process:

Those who have received from God the gift of faith in Christ, through the church, should be admitted with liturgical rites to the catechumenate which is not merely an exposition of dogmatic truths and norms of morality, but a period of formation in the entire Christian life, an apprenticeship of suitable duration, during which the disciples will be joined to Christ their teacher. The catechumens should be properly initiated into the mystery of salvation and the practice of the evangelical virtues, and they should be introduced into the life of faith, liturgy and charity of the people of God by successive sacred rites.

Then, having been delivered from the powers of darkness through the sacraments of Christian initiation, and having died, been buried, and risen with Christ, they receive the Spirit of adoption of children and celebrate with the whole people of God the memorial of the Lord's death and resurrection.

It is desirable that the liturgy of Lent and Paschal time should be restored in such a way that it will serve to prepare the hearts of catechumens for the celebration of the Paschal Mystery, at whose solemn ceremonies they are reborn to Christ in baptism.

This Christian initiation, which takes place during the catechumenate, should not be left entirely to the priests and catechists, but should be the concern of the whole Christian community, especially of the sponsors, so that from the beginning the catechumens will feel that they belong to the People of God. Since the life of the church is apostolic, the catechumens must learn to cooperate actively in the building up of the church and in its work of evangelization, both by the example of their lives and the profession of their faith.

The juridical status of catechumens should be clearly defined in the new Code of Canon Law. Since they have already joined the church they are already of the household of Christ and are quite frequently already living a life of faith, hope and charity (DCMA 14).

They even go on to suggest that the newest members of the church should be instructed in ecumenical sensitivity:

> The ecumenical spirit should be nourished among neophytes; they must appreciate that their brothers and sisters who believe in Christ are disciples of Christ and, having been reborn in baptism, share in many of the blessings of the people of God (DCMA 15).

The Council Fathers clearly saw the reestablishment of the catechumenate as an important goal, so much so that they declared that bishops "should take steps to reestablish or to improve the adult catechumenate" (*Decree on the Pastoral Office of Bishops in the Church* 14). They understood that those preparing for baptism, especially adults, needed to experience the grace of God through successive rites that would lead to full initiation into Christ. The process was to be Christocentric—centered on a relationship of faith in Christ. The process was to involve not only catechists and clergy but also the whole people of God. While uncertain what the process would actually look like, the bishops harkened back to earlier models of Christian initiation by using a vocabulary that was almost completely unknown to all but those who had studied liturgical or church history.

While not explicitly mentioning mystagogy in its constitutions, decrees, or declarations, the Council set the stage for its development as it describes the focus of Lent:

> Lent is marked by two themes, the baptismal and the penitential. By recalling or preparing for baptism and by repentance, this season disposes the faithful, as they more diligently listen to the word of God and devote themselves to prayer, to celebrate the paschal mystery. The baptismal and penitential aspects of Lent are to be given greater prominence in both the liturgy and liturgical catechesis. Hence:

a. More use is to be made of the baptismal features proper to the Lenten liturgy; some of those from an earlier era are to be restored as may seem advisable (CSL 109).

This emphasis on the baptismal nature of Lent was the first step on the rediscovery of the baptismal nature of Easter as well. It is this emphasis on baptism that led to the rebirth of mystagogy in the church toward the end of the second millennium.

The ideas behind this reform began to be debated long before the Council. There were several attempts to reestablish adult baptism as the norm and the catechumenate as the process for initiation, especially in France after World War II (Kavanagh 86–87). These discussions and experiments led the Council to reexamine the baptismal practices of the church as they gathered to look for ways to reinvigorate the church.

The *Rite of Christian Initiation of Adults*: The Provisional Text (1974)[33]

After completing the initial reform of the sacramentary and lectionary, the Congregation for Divine Worship, following up on the instructions issued by the Council, published the *Ordo Initiationis Christianae Adultorum*.[34] It took another two years for the International Commission on English in the Liturgy to publish an "interim or provisional" text in English.[35]

The *General Introduction* of the *Rite of Christian Initiation*[36] starts with references to adult initiation, mentioning the baptism of infants or children not as the norm but as an adaptation of the adult process. This is a major shift from the liturgical practice prior to Vatican II.

From the very beginning, the Rite uses the language of conversion in new ways. It speaks of "the path of faith and conversion" (RCIA 1974, 2), "the spiritual journey," "stages and steps," "forward through a gateway or up another step" (RCIA 1974, 5), and "pastoral formation" (RCIA 1974, 19). All of these images would seem strange to one who was more familiar with the rubrical and juridical nature of previous ritual books.

The process of steps and stages, envisioned by the *Rite of Christian Initiation of Adults*, was, at least in part, modeled after the fourth-century catechumenal processes described earlier in this chapter.[37]

The Rite described initiation as a continuous process made up of a series of four periods with three steps between the periods:

Period 1: The period of inquiry, evangelization, and precatechumenate

Step 1: The rite of becoming catechumens

Period 2: The catechumenate

Step 2: The rite of election or enrollment of names

Period 3: The period of purification and enlightenment

Step 3: The celebration of the sacraments of initiation

Period 4: The period of postbaptismal catechesis or mystagogia

Each of the steps is a public ritual, a celebration of the local church. Each of the periods includes appropriate catechesis for candidates at that stage of the process. Additional rituals, such as dismissals from the Sunday assembly, celebrations of the word of God, blessings, anointing, scrutinies, and presentations of the Creed and the Lord's Prayer are also part of Christian initiation. While each of the periods of adult initiation had disappeared during the preceding millennium, remnants of the ritual stages remained in the liturgical practices of the church.[38]

Much is said about the steps and other rituals in the Rite. There are, however, few explicit descriptions of the kinds of catechesis that ought to be part of the process. The Rite, however, does describe the goals of the initiation process as follows:

[The] candidates are to be grounded in the basic fundamentals of the spiritual life and Christian teachings (RCIA 1974, 15).

A fitting formation ... leads the catechumen to a suitable knowledge of dogma and precepts and also to an intimate understanding of the mystery of salvation (RCIA 1974, 19.1).

[The] catechumens will learn to pray to God more easily, to witness to the faith, to be constant in the expectation of Christ in all things, to follow supernatural inspiration in their deeds, and to exercise charity toward neighbors to the point of self-renunciation (RCIA 1974, 19.2).

There were, however, no descriptions as to how these goals are to be met. The content and methods of catechesis are never made clear in the Rite. The Rite itself presumes that the rituals will teach, that the experiences of the church at prayer with the candidates will reveal the faith of the church. The ancient maxim *lex orandi, lex credendi*[39] seems to function as a foundational principle for the entire process. For a church so closely tied to educational practice—especially in the United States, where only government operates more schools—this is a radical departure from the methods of catechesis in use prior to Vatican II.[40] Thus a new vision of catechesis is proclaimed,[41] one in which experience is taken more seriously and in which learning occurs on several levels. The Rite sees conversion as much more than simply an intellectual experience. There is more to faith than intellectual knowledge of the church's doctrines and dogmas. One does not only come to know about God in new ways but also enters into a new relationship with God. Catechesis and ritual open one to a conversion that involves the whole person, a conversion that affects the thoughts, feelings, relationships, and behaviors of the one who is being initiated. The initiation process is not primarily about religious education, but about faith formation.[42]

The Rite also proclaimed a new vision of church, a vision first articulated in the Vatican II documents, especially the *Dogmatic Constitution on the Church* (1964) and the *Pastoral Constitution on the Church in the Modern World* (1965).[43] The Rite presumes that parishes are places where "the example and support of sponsors and godparents and the whole community of the faithful" (RCIA 1974, 19.2) will assist the catechumens in their learning. This participation of "the whole community of the faithful" in the initiation of new members could be seen as a radical departure from the days when the baptism of adults was done quietly on a Saturday morning with only a few family or friends present. The Rite makes this point clear when it states the following:

> The people of God, represented by the local church, should always understand and show that the initiation of adults is its concern and the business of all the baptized.
>
> Therefore the community must always be ready to fulfill its apostolic vocation by giving help to those who need Christ. ... [The] community must help the candidates and catechumens throughout their whole period of initiation, during the precatechumenate, the catechumenate, and the period of postbaptismal catechesis or mystagogia (RCIA 1974, 41).

This, too, is a major change from the recent practice in which only the candidate and the priest giving instructions had any role in the preparation for baptism.

The role of the godparents or sponsors is much more important as well. They do not merely witness the baptismal ritual, but they also fully participate in every ritual, from the rite of becoming catechumens[44] through celebration of the Masses for the neophytes during the Easter season and beyond.

> It is [the godparent's] responsibility to show the catechumen in a friendly way the place of the Gospel in [one's] own life and in society, to sustain [the candidate] in [moments of] doubts and anxieties, to give public witness for [the candidate], and to watch over the progress of [the candidate's] baptismal life. ... [This] responsibility remains important when the neophyte has received the sacraments and needs to be helped to remain faithful to [the] baptismal promises (RCIA 1974, 43).

The Rite also called for a period of postbaptismal catechesis or mystagogia (RCIA 1974, 37–40, 235–239; see Appendix 1). Unlike the postbaptismal mystagogy of the fourth century, which lasted but one week, the Rite called for a period of fifty days, from Easter to Pentecost. The experience of the sacraments itself would lead to "a fuller, more fruitful understanding of the 'mysteries'" (RCIA 1974, 38). This would be especially true because the Rite envisioned the Eucharist as a completely new experience for the neophytes.[45] The Rite envisions mystagogical catechesis taking place within the Sunday celebration of the Eucharist throughout the Easter season. Rather than gathering every day during Easter week, as they did in the fourth century, neophytes and their sponsors would gather in a place of honor in the midst of the Sunday assembly for the eight Sundays of the Easter season. This presumes that mystagogical homilies will be preached at these celebrations, homilies in which connections will be made between the sacramental experiences of the neophytes and the sacred Scriptures so that a deeper understanding of the mysteries of salvation might emerge.

The Rite likewise called for the bishop to preside (and presumably preach) at both the rite of election (at the beginning of Lent) and a Mass for the neophytes (sometime during their first year of membership in the church). Thus the Rite envisioned that the neophytes would have experienced the support, not only of their sponsors (or godparents) and catechists, but also the support and encouragement of all the faithful, including the deacons, priests, and the bishop of the local church.

The vision of the Rite also included a deep respect for the faith background of those who are coming to the Catholic Church. Persons already baptized in the Christian faith were not to be re-baptized unless there was a serious doubt as to the validity of the baptism they received (GI 4). The previous practice was to baptize almost all those who came from some other Christian church, at least conditionally, on the assumption that their previous baptism may have been possibly invalid.

The Rite likewise acknowledged that people come with varying degrees of religious maturity and thus made provisions for a shorter process for some candidates.[46] This new vision of the Rite exemplified a deep respect for each individual and his or her religious background.

The 1974 edition also declared that children who have reached the age of reason are neither infants nor adults, and a separate process was described for them. Based on the adult rite and including the same stages and periods, the rituals for children were adapted to their needs and level of maturity. No longer would children be treated either as big infants or as small adults.

The *Rite of Christian Initiation of Adults*: The Adaptations for the United States of America (1988)

In the decree by Archbishop John L. May, at the very beginning of the published text of the 1988 adaptations of the *Rite of Christian Initiation of Adults* for the church in the U.S.A., the Rite was called "mandatory," ending any confusion concerning the "provisional" nature of the 1974 edition. The *Code of Canon Law* had previously made this clear when it stated the following:

> An adult who intends to receive baptism is to be admitted to the catechumenate and, to the extent possible, be led through the several stages to sacramental initiation, in accord with the order of initiation adapted by the conference of bishops and the special norms published by them (CCL 851, 1).

After more than ten years of experience with the Rite, the Bishops' Committee on Liturgy, National Conference of Catholic Bishops, prepared this special edition of the *Rite of Christian Initiation of Adults*, with adaptations particular to the dioceses of the United States of America. New translations of a slightly revised *editio typico*[47] of the *Rite of Christian Initiation of Adults* were made by the International Commission on English in the Liturgy. The structure of the presentation was rearranged "in the interest of pastoral utility and convenience" (RCIA foreword). The previously separate rite of reception into the full communion of the Catholic Church (for those who were baptized in another Christian ecclesial community) was also integrated into this new edition.

Additional rituals were added because of the frequent experience within the American church of ministering with persons who were already baptized but for whom the catechesis and some of the rituals of the Rite might be pastorally appropriate. These new rituals include (see RCIA table of contents):

- Optional Rites for Baptized but Uncatechized Adults

  - Rite of Welcoming Candidates
  - Rite of Sending the Candidates for Recognition by the Bishop and for the Call to Continuing Conversion
  - Rite of Calling the Candidates to Continuing Conversion
  - Penitential Rite (Scrutiny)

- Additional (Combined) Rites

  - Celebration of the Rite of Acceptance into the Order of Catechumens and of the Rite of Welcoming Baptized but Previously Uncatechized Adults Who Are Preparing for Confirmation and/or Eucharist or Reception into the Full Communion of the Catholic Church
  - Parish Celebration for Sending Catechumens for election and Candidates for Recognition by the Bishop
  - Celebration of the Rite of election of Catechumens and of the Call to Continuing Conversion of Candidates Who Are Preparing for Confirmation and/or Eucharist or Reception into the Full Communion of the Catholic Church
  - Celebration at the Easter Vigil of the Sacraments of Initiation and of the Rite of Reception into the Full Communion of the Catholic Church.

These additional rituals widen the church's vision of Christian initiation to include all those who seek to complete their initiation in the Catholic Church, especially those who would benefit from an experience similar to the catechumenate.[48] While the 1974 edition stated that "some of the rites belonging to the catechumenate may be used if desired" (RCIA 1974, 302), the 1988 edition offers specific rituals adapted for those "adults who were baptized as infants either as Roman Catholics or as members of another Christian community but did not receive further catechetical formation, nor consequently, the sacraments of confirmation and eucharist" (RCIA 400).

By rearranging and providing new translations of the instructions concerning mystagogy, the adaptation for the church in United States of America makes it clear that mystagogy is liturgy.[49] It is the work of the whole community.

> [Mystagogy] is a time for the community and the neophytes to grow in deepening their grasp of the paschal mystery and in making it part of their lives through meditation on the Gospel, sharing in the eucharist, and doing the works of charity. To strengthen the neophytes as they begin to walk in newness of life, the community of the faithful, their godparents, and their pastors [parish priests] should give them thoughtful and friendly help (RCIA 244).

> The period of postbaptismal catechesis is of great significance for both the neophytes and the rest of the faithful. Through it the neophytes, with the help of their godparents, should experience a full and joyful welcome into the community and enter into closer ties with the other faithful. The faithful, in turn, should derive from it a renewal of inspiration and of outlook (RCIA 246).

Additionally, the National Conference of Catholic Bishops approved the *National Statutes for the Catechumenate*, which were published as an appendix to the Rite.[50] The national statutes seek to make some of the instructions in the introductions of the Rite clearer. These included three specific statutes concerning mystagogy, one of which expands the vision of mystagogy in the United States of America when it says the following:

> After the immediate mystagogy or postbaptismal catechesis during the Easter season, the program for the neophytes should extend until the anniversary of Christian initiation, with at least monthly assemblies of the neophytes for their deeper Christian formation and incorporation into the full life of the Christian community (NSC 24).

These monthly assemblies for the neophytes are a completely new addition to the initiation process. The church's vision of postbaptismal mystagogy has expanded over time as the period grew from one week (in the fourth century), to fifty days (in RCIA 1974), to a year-long program following the immediate mystagogy of the Easter season (in NSC). It has grown to include monthly gatherings in addition to the Masses for the neophytes, where mystagogy was previously seen as taking place.

The Catechism of the Catholic Church

The *Catechism of the Catholic Church* describes the relationship of catechesis and liturgy as follows:

> "The liturgy is the summit toward which the activity of the Church is directed; it is also the font from which all her power flows." It is therefore the privileged place for catechizing the People of God. "Catechesis is intrinsically linked with the whole of liturgical and sacramental activity, for it is in the sacraments, especially the Eucharist, that Christ Jesus works in fullness for the transformation of [human beings]" (CCC 1074).

> Liturgical catechesis aims to initiate people into the mystery of Christ (It is "mystagogy.") by proceeding from the visible to the invisible, from the sign to the thing signified, from the "sacraments" to the "mysteries" (CCC 1075).

Like the preaching of the ancient mystagogues, the *Catechism* reveals a vision of mystagogy that includes catechesis that is grounded in the liturgy and helps the neophytes make connections between their experience of the liturgy and mysteries of salvation. The Scriptures and the traditions of the church are also seen as essential elements in this process.

Some Conclusions

The following theological principles offer a foundation for a contemporary understanding of Christian initiation and mystagogy in particular. None of these principles is new, but each has been nuanced and given new emphasis since Vatican II.

1. The church is the people of God. Thus the whole process of Christian initiation is the work of the whole people of God. The

members of the assembly have a major role to play in the initiation of new members.

2. The Eucharist is the source and summit of the Christian life. Thus, the focus or goal of Christian initiation is not simply baptism but the ongoing experience of the paschal mystery celebrated in the Eucharist. Initiation does not end with baptism, but through the Eucharist, Christians are continually initiated into the saving mystery of Christ.

3. Christ is really present in the gathering of assembly, in the proclamation of the word, in the celebration of the mysteries (i.e., sacraments), in the ministry of those in positions of leadership in the community, and in the bread broken and the wine poured. Thus the process of initiation takes seriously all the various ways in which Christ reveals himself to his people.

4. Faith is a way of life, a relationship with God and God's people. Faith is not simply an intellectual knowledge of a collection of doctrinal statements. Thus the initiation process is directed toward a life of faith, not simply an intellectual assent to faith's doctrinal content. The relationship it fosters is much wider than a personal relationship with Jesus Christ. It includes a relationship with the whole Body of Christ, the whole Christian people.

5. Actions speak louder than words. This applies to the initiation process in that our liturgical and ministerial actions often speak louder than what we say in our catechetical sessions. Thus, good liturgy[51] is as important as, or more important than, good catechesis.

6. Catechesis is intimately related to the liturgical experience. Catechesis is reflection on the liturgical experience—both word proclaimed and the ritual enacted—whether it takes place before or after the experience. Mystagogical catechesis begins with reflection on what was heard, seen, felt, sensed, or experienced in the liturgy.[52]

7. Eucharist leads to mission. The experience of the paschal mystery leads to service for the sake of the reign of God. Thus, throughout the initiation process, the catechumens, Elect, and neophytes are called to mission.[53]

8. Sponsors and godparents walk with catechumens, the Elect, and neophytes throughout the journey of faith. The initiation process enables, encourages, and nourishes them as they share their lives with those they are sponsoring.

9. Deacons, priests, and bishops have significant roles in the process of initiation. These roles should not be limited to presiding at the rites. Thus, opportunities for catechumens, the Elect, and neophytes to meet with the clergy are important to the initiation process.

10. Each person's faith journey is respected. Thus, the initiation process takes into account the varying experiences and needs of the candidates as the process is implemented.[54]

11. Mystagogy helps the neophytes (and the faithful), to integrate their new experience of sharing in the Eucharist with the whole of their lives. Thus, mystagogical homilies, which break open both the word and ritual, are preached in initiating communities.

Chapter 4

A Conversation with Present Practices and the Church's Vision of Mystagogy

As the search for an effective mystagogy progresses, this chapter continues the conversation begun in the introduction of this book.[1] It is a conversation we have been preparing for since the beginning—a conversation between twenty-five recent neophytes,[2] four ancient mystagogues, the contemporary Rite, and ourselves. It is a conversation that has already led us to several insights about an effective mystagogy, which will be part of this chapter.

In Chapters 1 and 2, we were introduced to and analyzed the practices of some recent neophytes. In the third chapter, we examined the church's vision of mystagogy as found in the preachings of four ancient mystagogues and the *Rite of Christian Initiation of Adults*. The preliminary conclusions drawn from these reflections have become the sources for and the participants in our conversation in this chapter. Each participant in the conversation comes from a different time and place. Each has expressed convictions from different points of view and in different forms. Recent neophytes shared the stories of their conversion. Ancient mystagogues preached to the neophytes and the faithful in their day and in their local communities. The Rite is a ritual book that is meant to guide ministers in local communities as they celebrate the movement of God in the lives of those who are being initiated into the Catholic Church today. Though very different in their methods and approaches, each conversation partner has pointed us toward similar conclusions as we have searched for an effective mystagogy. Now we bring these three conversation partners together.

The conclusions found at the end of our analysis of the present practices (see pages 70–71), the preaching of the ancient mystagogues (see pages 92–93) and our reflection on the contemporary Rite (see pages 105–107) form the "flow,"[3] which points our conversation in a particular direction. The three conversation partners will, like the river's flow, guide the conversation as it moves toward some conclusions and recommendations for a contemporary mystagogical practice that will be found in the final chapter of this book.

As this chapter progresses, the conversation will begin with a discussion of three significant questions:

1. What are the goals of mystagogy?

2. What is the context in which mystagogy occurs?

3. Who are the significant people involved in an effective mystagogy?

Each of the conversation partners will add something to the discussion of these questions. None will provide a complete answer, but together they point the way. Like any conversation, each participant takes the lead from time to time. One speaks louder and clearer on one subject or another, but all have something to contribute to the dialogue and the direction of our searching.

In Search of ... ?

Before examining the currents, flows, topics, or questions that form the basic structure of this chapter, let us look at the conversation itself and where it seems to be heading. When I began my research, the focus of the investigation was the search for an effective mystagogy. However, as that search progressed, it became clear that an effective mystagogy could not entirely be separated from an effective initiation process. The search for an effective mystagogy could not be isolated from the search for an effective conversion experience. The whole process needed to be considered. Our search for an effective mystagogy might in fact be called a search for an effective initiation experience.

When recent neophytes were asked to describe their experience of mystagogy, they could not help but describe the whole initiation process. They described the effects, not only of mystagogy, but of the entire initiation process. They reminisced about the various rituals they experienced and the persons who were important along the way. They talked about the ways in which the whole process was a conversation between their lives, the sacred Scriptures, and the rites of the church. They described their experiences of the real presence of Christ in the assembly gathered, in the word proclaimed, and in the ministers ministering long before they understood or even heard of the terminology, the theology, or the experience of real presence in the Eucharist.[4]

Every one of the great fourth-century mystagogues also has surviving catechetical sermons or instructions.[5] There seems to be a close connection between their catechetical preaching and their mystagogical preaching. While the mystagogical preaching is intimately related to the celebration of baptism, confirmation,[6] and Eucharist, the same styles and methods are generally used in the catechetical sermons that usually focus on the Lord's Prayer and the Creed. In both types of preaching, the Scriptures are used to help the listeners discover the deeper meaning of the text or the ritual— "developing an understanding of the mystery" (Mazza 3) which lies behind, beneath, or beyond the text or ritual. The consistent use of particular methods by each of the ancient mystagogues demonstrates an essential unity between their catechetical and mystagogical preaching.

While the Rite itself speaks of postbaptismal catechesis or mystagogy, the two terms are not synonymous. The period of postbaptismal catechesis is a specific time, the weeks and months that follow the celebration of the sacraments of initiation. Mystagogy, however, is a catechetical method of reflecting on experience leading "from the visible to the invisible, from the sign to the thing signified, from the 'sacraments' to the 'mysteries'" (CCC 1075). This process is evident during the period of evangelization or precatechumenate when that initial evangelization takes place and the candidates reflect on the presence of God in their life experiences, during the catechumenate when they reflect on the mystery of God revealed in the sacred Scriptures proclaimed in the Sunday liturgy, and during the period of postbaptismal catechesis when they reflect on the mystery of God experienced through the signs and symbols of the sacraments.

The Rite says, "The whole initiation must bear a markedly paschal character" (RCIA 8). One might also say that the whole initiation process ought to be mystagogical. The whole process should lead from experience to encounter with mystery. I will say more about this in the final chapter. For now, let us simply acknowledge that the search for an effective mystagogy is indeed the search for an effective initiation process, which is mystagogical throughout.

This insight would seem to indicate that the questions this chapter seeks to answer need to be rephrased to include the whole of the initiation experience. While the conversation will continue to focus on mystagogy, it must be open to the whole process. Thus, our questions for our conversation might be restated as the following:

1. What are the goals of an initiation process that is mystagogical throughout?

2. What is the context in which an authentically mystagogical initiation occurs?

3. Who are the significant people involved in an authentically mystagogical initiation process?

These are the questions this chapter will seek to answer.

What Are the Goals of an Initiation Process That Is Mystagogical Throughout?

Knowing the expected outcomes or the hoped-for results of any process is essential to planning well. When one knows the goals, one can aim for them. The ways in which some parish initiation processes implement the Rite seem to be aimed at baptism alone, but the witness of recent neophytes discussed in Chapter 2 indicates that "the goal of initiation is living the Christian life" (see conclusion 11 on page 71 and the discussion that follows on page 71ff.). This is confirmed by the preaching of the late-fourth-century mystagogues who often emphasize that "a moral life is the only adequate response to God's salvation" (see conclusion 6 on page 92). Conclusions from an analysis of the church's contemporary documents about initiation likewise verify this (see conclusion 4 on page 106). Together, these witnesses begin to answer our question stated above. They indicate that among the hoped-for results of the initiation experience are new behaviors and new relationships that enable a person to live the Christian life. We will look at each of these in turn.

New Behaviors

Hippolytus looked for behavioral changes in the lives of those who were to be baptized. Persons engaged in certain professions or relationships that were considered immoral were to avoid them or be rejected by the church before they even began the formal initiation process (AT 16).[7] Each of the late-fourth-century mystagogues also mentioned specific professions or behaviors that a new Christian ought to avoid. John Chrysostom mentioned "the vanity of worldly goods" (BI 8, 11–15), swearing (BI 9, 36–47; 10, 18–20), taking oaths (BI 10, 21–30), wearing jewelry (BI 12, 18–20) and numerous others. Egeria wrote that the bishop asks if those seeking initiation are "drunkard[s] or boaster[s]."

Not only are some behaviors to be avoided, but others need to develop. Hippolytus examined "those who are to receive baptism" prior to being initiated. He asked these questions:

> Have they lived good lives when they were catechumens? Have they honored the widows? Have they visited the sick? Have they done every kind of good work? (AT 20).

He likewise instructed his readers that an initiated person "shall hasten to do good works and to please God and to conduct himself rightly, being zealous for the church, doing what he has learnt and advancing in piety" (AT 21). Egeria reported that the bishop asked the neighbors of the catechumens, "Is this person leading a good life?

Does he respect his parents?" (ET 45.3). In his *Mystagogic Catechesis*, Cyril of Jerusalem exhorted his listeners to "walk in newness of life" (MC 2, 8). Shortly before being initiated, John Chrysostom instructed the catechumens as follows:

> [T]hrough the kindness of God, you will be called a Christian and one of the faithful. ... Soon you will put on Christ. You must act and deliberate in all things with the knowledge that [Christ] is everywhere with you (BI 1, 44).

He also admonished both "the neophytes and [those] who have long since been initiated" (BI 3, 20) to "show to all, by the discipline of our lives, the power of [the One] who dwells within us" (BI 4, 18).

> Let your virtue, ... and your well-disciplined conduct and the uprightness of your deeds move those who behold you to praise the common Master of us all. I exhort you: let each one of you be eager to live life with such exactness that prayer of worship may ascent to the Master from all who behold you (BI 4, 22).

It seems that our ancestors in faith were looking for specific new behaviors as they examined those who were about to be initiated. They believed that the Christian faithful behaved differently from others in their society. They looked for behavior motivated by Gospel charity—by love of God and love of neighbor. They also believed that these behaviors could be identified and recognized.

Today, the Rite, too, questions the behavior of those about to be initiated. During the rite of election, the godparents are expected to testify that the candidate has "endeavored to follow [Christ's] commands" (RCIA 131A) and has "responded to [God's] word and begun to walk in God's presence" (RCIA 131B). These are not meant to be mere ritual statements, because the Rite instructs the following:

> To exclude any semblance of mere formality from the rite, there should be a deliberation prior to [the] celebration [of the rite of election] to decide on the catechumen's suitableness (RCIA 122).

This suitableness is based on the experience of the catechumenate, during which they were to "become familiar with the Christian way of life," were to have been helped "by the example and support of sponsors, godparents and the entire Christian community," and were to have learned "to bear witness to the faith, ... to practice love of neighbor, even at the cost of self-renunciation" (RCIA 75.2). The exorcisms and scrutinies, too, presume that the Elect are open to changing their behaviors. They presume that with the grace of God one can "uncover, then heal all that is weak, defective, or sinful in the hearts of the Elect, [and] bring out, then strengthen all that is upright, strong, and good" (RCIA 141).

Likewise, the Rite describes the period of postbaptismal catechesis as "a time for the community and the neophytes to grow in deepening their grasp of the paschal mystery and in making it part of their lives" (RCIA 244). It also states that "out of this experience, ... they derive a new perception of the faith, of the church and of the world" (RCIA 245). This new perception undoubtedly has behavioral and relational consequences, because the Rite warns that "the newly converted often experience division and separations, but they also taste the joy that God gives without measure" (RCIA 75.2). This warning in some ways echoes the Gospel predictions that "you will be hated by all because of my name" (Lk 21:17; see also Mt 10:22, 24:9; Mk 13:13).

While this warning only concerns the negative impact conversion might have on relationships, many recent neophytes spoke of the positive impact conversion had on many of their relationships. Several of the recent neophytes I interviewed identified specific behaviors that had changed in their lives. These included the ways they related to their spouses, children, and coworkers. Family members, neighbors, and coworkers noticed these changes. The changes included being less anxious and more patient and understanding. They were less likely to become angry over minor things. They treated others with more respect and kindness. Several of the recent neophytes were able to reconcile with people from whom they previously had been estranged. Some of the recent neophytes also changed careers as a result of their conversion. They felt that they could no longer work for certain companies and practice the justice demanded by their newfound faith.

The experience of recent neophytes, as well as the church's ancient and contemporary witness, proclaim clearly that the initiation process ought to and does affect the behavior and relationships of those who are initiated into the saving mysteries of Christ.

One could say that the goal of Christian initiation that is truly mystagogical—borrowing words spoken during the distribution of the ashes on Ash Wednesday—is to assist persons to continually "turn away from sin and be faithful to the Gospel."[8]

New Relationships

In addition to the changes that occur in the previously existing personal relationships of the neophytes at home, at school, at work, and in the parish, new relationships are also established. Any initiation is about establishing a new relationship with some group of people or organization. Christian initiation is about being brought into the Christian community, about joining God's chosen people, and about becoming a member of the Body of Christ. An authentically mystagogical initiation process thus instills in the neophyte a sense of belonging—belonging to God and to the church.

The recent neophytes I interviewed indicated that they were looking to belong to something greater than themselves (see pages 59–60). Some ministers of initiation believe that many people cease participating in the life of the church after being fully initiated, because while the candidates experience a sense of belonging during the initiation process, they do not have a similar experience in regard to the larger Christian community once initiated (see page 11).

Christian Initiation: General Introduction speaks about these new relationships when it states the following:

> [The initiated] receive the Spirit of filial adoption and are part of the entire people of God in the celebration of the Lord's death and resurrection.
>
> Baptism incorporates us into Christ and forms us into God's people. ... [It] brings us to the dignity of adopted children, a new creation through water and the Holy Spirit. Hence we are called and are indeed the children of God (GI 1–2).

[Baptism's] recipients are incorporated into the church and are built up together in the Spirit into a house where God lives, into a holy nation and royal priesthood (GI 4).

Baptism ... makes us sharers in God's own life (GI 5).

At the rite of election, those who are to be initiated are called "[God's] adopted children ... chosen ones ... true children of the promise" (RCIA 135A). During the celebration of the sacraments of initiation, the neophytes are addressed as those who "have become a new creation and have clothed [them]selves in Christ" (RCIA 229). As those who "have been enlightened by Christ," they are also called "children of the light" (RCIA 230). They are "born again in Christ, ... have become members of Christ and of his priestly people" (RCIA 233). In all these ways, they have established new relationships both with God and the church.

The late-fourth-century mystagogues also used numerous images to describe these new relationships. The neophytes have become the spouse of Christ (BI 1, 1–18), citizens of the city of God (BH 6, 23–27) and of the reign or kingdom of God. They "have 'put on Christ,'... have become conformed to the Son of God, ... 'share in Christ' ... have become anointed ones" (MC 3, 1). They entered the holy of holies (MC 1, 11). They participated "in resurrection and in the good things that emanate from it" (BH 6, 22). "Just as the Holy Spirit is in [their] heart, so too Christ is in [their] heart" (OS 6, 6). They have been described as those "who have ... been inscribed as citizens of heaven, who have been invited to this spiritual banquet and are about to enjoy the benefits of the royal table" (BI 4, 6). In these ways, the neophytes are described as belonging to something larger than themselves, something beyond mere human nature, something divine. This is clearly a new kind of relationship.

The Rite, too, focuses on new relationships as a goal of the period of postbaptismal catechesis when it states the following:

Through [the period of postbaptismal catechesis] the neophytes, with the help of their godparents, should experience a full and joyful welcome into the community and enter into closer ties with the other faithful (RCIA 246).

Neophytes should thus experience a new relationship to the whole Christian community that gathers in the parish. An effective initiation process, as such, enables neophytes to experience a sense of belonging to both God and the church.

Living the Christian Life

Whether we talk to recent neophytes, ancient mystagogues, or contemporary critics of the *Rite of Christian Initiation of Adults*, a clear goal is in mind for the initiation process. The goal is not baptism. Nor is it simply sharing in the Sunday Eucharist. From the teachings of the fourth-century mystagogues to this very day, the goal is to enable people to live as citizens of the reign of God. It is the goal set out for all believers from the very beginning of the Gospel. It is the same mission that Jesus himself handed on to the disciples as expressed in the Gospels:

> "Go into the whole world and proclaim the Gospel to every creature" (Mk 16:15).

It is the Good News that Jesus proclaimed:

> "The kingdom of God is at hand" (Mk 1:15).

One lives the Christian life as a witness to the reign of God as John Chrysostom proclaims:

> For the future, all of you, both you who have just deserved the gift and all who have already reaped for yourselves the benefit of His munificence, must make the excellence of your conduct visible to all, after the fashion of a torch, you must illumine those who look upon you (BI 7, 24).

We proclaim that reign whenever the hungry are fed, the thirsty given drink, the stranger welcomed, the naked clothed, the ill cared for, and the imprisoned visited (cf. Mt 25:31–46). The fourth-century mystagogues called the neophytes to a moral life as the only adequate response to God's salvation celebrated in the sacraments of initiation.

118

What the Rite says about the catechumenate might be said about the whole initiation experience, it is quite simply "aimed at training ... in the Christian life" (RCIA 75).

Living the Christian life is about more than ritual behaviors. While the ancient mystagogues and the current Rite ask about a candidate's behavior in regard to participation in the ritual life of the church, they ask about much more. Much of the previous discuss about behaviors that result from—or are expected to result from—an effective initiation experience are appropriate to reflect on again in this regard.

During the rite of election, the bishop asks the godparents the following questions (RCIA 131B) about those who are to be chosen for the Easter sacraments:

Have they faithfully listened to God's word proclaimed by the church?

Have they shared the company of their Christian brothers and sisters and joined with them in prayer?

He also asks about the lives they are leading:

Have they responded to that word and begun to walk in God's presence?

These same kinds of questions were asked during the rites celebrated by Hippolytus and witnessed by Egeria. The preaching of Cyril of Jerusalem, John Chrysostom, Ambrose of Milan, and Theodore of Mopsuestia often encouraged and challenged the neophytes to live the faith into which they were about to be or had recently been initiated. Specific behaviors are mentioned in the section on behaviors above.

According to the Rite, mystagogical preaching today is meant to introduce the neophytes

into a fuller and more effective understanding of the mysteries through the Gospel message they have learned and above all through their experience of the sacraments they have received. For they have truly been renewed in mind, tasted more deeply the sweetness of God's word, received the fellowship of the Holy Spirit, and grown to know the goodness of the Lord. Out of this experience, which belongs to Christians and increases as it is lived, they derive a new perception of the faith, of the church, and of the world (RCIA 245).

They are "to grow in deepening their grasp of the paschal mystery and in making it part of their lives" and "to begin to walk in newness of life" (RCIA 244). These are all indications that one of the goals of Christian initiation is living the Christian life.

If the goals of an effective initiation process include new behaviors and new relationships with God and the church, and the living of the Christian life, then the focus of mystagogy must be more than an analysis of the experience of sacraments of initiation. The late-fourth-century mystagogues did not simply analyze the various elements of the rite in order to help the neophytes have a clearer mental image of what had happened. Their preaching about the various parts of the ritual were not simply aimed at looking back at what had already happened. It was motivated by a belief that a clear understanding of what had already happened would lead the neophytes to a new way of living in the days, weeks, and years ahead. It was also meant to motivate the neophytes to experience the Eucharist as the place where the nourishment needed to live that life could be found.

What Is the Context in Which an Authentically Mystagogical Initiation Process Occurs?

Initiation always occurs within the context of a particular community gathered together. Initiation is never an isolated event. One is always initiated into a group of people, whether it is a small or a large community. Christian initiation takes place within the context of the Christian community. Most of the rituals found within the *Rite of Christian Initiation of Adults* are celebrated within the Sunday assembly. Even those rituals that are not celebrated in that context are celebrated within the context of the celebrations of the word. Christian initiation takes place within a liturgical community, a community gathered to offer prayer and praise to God. This context sets the stage for the process and has a profound influence on how the process is experienced.

Our three dialogue partners seem to indicate that the context of an authentically mystagogical initiation process is the local Christian community, a community that gathers around the eucharistic table and is formed by the word of God.

The Local Christian Community

The recent neophytes I interviewed described the local community as a welcoming community—a place where they felt at home the very first time they set foot in the church. It was this sense of welcome or of being at home that often contributed to their initial seeking to be initiated into the community. Many neophytes also reported that the experience of the rite of election and several other encounters with persons both in the local community and in the local diocese helped them understand they were being initiated into something larger than the local parish.

In each of the parishes I visited while creating an effective mystagogy, the local community sponsored several community outreach programs. The parishes were active in the area of social justice, offering assistance to persons in need not only in their local community but also beyond it. The local parish was not isolated from the rest of the church or the local area. It was not a closed community, but one that was open to persons of various backgrounds. While all of the communities were located in areas where the population was primarily European American, there were persons of color in every worshiping community I visited.

The Rite itself speaks of the central role of the local community, listing it as the first of the ministries and offices involved in the Christian initiation of adults:

The people of God, as represented by the local church, should understand and show by their concern that the initiation of adults is the responsibility of all the baptized. Therefore the community must always be fully prepared in the pursuit of its apostolic vocation to give help to those who are searching for Christ. In the various circumstances of daily life, even as in the apostolate, all the

121

followers of Christ have the obligation of preaching the faith according to their abilities. Hence, the entire community must help the candidates and the catechumens throughout the process of initiation (RCIA 9).

The Rite specifically calls on the local community to participate in the period of postbaptismal catechesis, saying this:

> During the period immediately after baptism, the faithful should take part in the Masses for neophytes, ... welcome the neophytes with open arms in charity, and help them to feel more at home in the community of the baptized (RCIA 9.5).

The participation of the whole community is presumed by the Rite when it states that mystagogy is "a time for the community and the neophytes together to grow" (RCIA 244) and that it "is of great significance for both the neophytes and the rest of the faithful" (RCIA 246).

Egeria spoke of how the many in the local community in Jerusalem came together for prayer with the candidates throughout the initiation process but spoke especially of how they gathered during Easter week "to hear the Mysteries" (ET 47.2). The community was so caught up in what was being preached that she exclaimed, "Indeed, the way [the bishop] expounds the mysteries and interprets them cannot fail to move his hearers" (ET 47.2).

There are indications throughout the mystagogical preaching of Cyril of Jerusalem, John Chrysostom, Ambrose of Milan, and Theodore of Mopsuestia that the neophytes were not alone when they heard these sermons. Likewise, in the catechetical preaching during Lent, these same preachers indicate that the larger community is gathered to hear again the message of salvation. The presence of the local community witnessed to the need for continuing conversion and offered encouragement to the catechumens and the neophytes in the local community.

It is in the local Christian community that all the faithful are continually called to mystagogical reflection—to recognizing the presence of God in the everyday experiences of life, in the word proclaimed, and in the bread broken and the wine shared. A community that is truly mystagogical is constantly open to conversion, and it is only in such a community that inquirers, catechumens, the Elect, neophytes, and all the Christian faithful can experience truly effective initiation into the saving mysteries of Christ.

Gathered at the Eucharistic Table

Vatican II called the Eucharist the source and summit of the Christian life. Ritually, the whole initiation process culminates in the celebration of the Eucharist, when the neophytes eat the bread of life and drink the cup of salvation and thus complete their initiation. The Eucharist is not, however, merely the end of the initiation process.

For many of the neophytes it was the experience of gathering around the eucharistic table that inspired them to seek initiation into the Christian community.[9] It is also while gathered for the Eucharist that most of the other rituals of the initiation process take place. Inquirers become catechumens at the Sunday Eucharist. Week after week, catechumens listen to the Scriptures proclaimed during the Liturgy of the Word, and the "community sends [them] forth to reflect more deeply upon the word of God which [they] have shared ... [until] the day when [they] will share fully in the Lord's Table" (RCIA 67B). They are sent for election, scrutinized, initiated, and hold places of honor during the Easter season within assembly. Even the minor exorcisms, blessings, and anointings generally take place within a liturgical context.[10]

From the day of their initiation on, it is at the Eucharist that the neophytes find their strength and encouragement. Of the three sacraments of initiation, only the Eucharist is celebrated over and over again. Once the neophytes have shared the Eucharist completely as the culmination of their initiation, they will share it every Sunday for the rest of their lives. The Eucharist becomes the repeatable celebration of initiation by which all are initiated more and more deeply into the mystery of God in Christ.

The description, in the Rite, of the neophytes' first sharing in the celebration of the Eucharist makes clear the importance of the Eucharist in the initiation process. It is "the culminating point in their Christian initiation. ... When in communion they receive the body that was given for us and the blood that was shed, the neophytes are strengthened in the gifts they have already received and are given a foretaste of the eternal banquet" (RCIA 217).

Furthermore, the Rite clearly centers postbaptismal mystagogy in the context of the Sunday Eucharist when it states the following:

> Since the distinctive spirit and power of the period of postbaptismal catechesis or mystagogy derive from the new, personal experience of the sacraments and of the community, its main setting is the so-called Masses for neophytes, that is, the Sunday Masses of the Easter season (RCIA 247).

The *National Statutes for the Catechumenate* again confirm the centrality of the Eucharist when they state this:

> Mystagogy should embrace a deepened understanding of the mysteries of baptism, confirmation, and the eucharist, and *especially of the eucharist as the continuing celebration of faith and conversion* (NSC 23; italics added).

While there is no indication that the mystagogical preaching of the late fourth century took place during the Eucharist, as it does today, the Eucharist is a major focus of that preaching.[11] Likewise, both the catechetical and mystagogical preaching took place within a liturgical setting (see conclusion 10 on page 93). The preaching on the Eucharist always occurred after its reception. The *disciplina arcani*[12] of the time did not permit any unbaptized person to be present when the Eucharist was celebrated, nor were the faithful to discuss what occurred or its meaning with the unbaptized.[13] Therefore, the neophytes knew little about the Eucharist until they had partaken in the sacrament. Thus the preaching during Easter week would have been the neophyte's first encounter with any description or explanation of the Eucharist.

Cyril of Jerusalem culminated his five *Mystagogic Catechesis* with two instructions on the Eucharist, clearly aimed at inspiring the neophytes to treasure the gift of the Eucharist. In his last instruction, he interprets the Lord's Prayer, connecting the bread of that prayer with the bread that "is absorbed into your whole system to the benefit of both soul and body" (MC 5, 15).[14] It is also "daily" bread, bread that is eaten not once, but over and over again. Cyril also instructs the neophytes on how to properly receive the Eucharist, clearly pointing to future celebrations of this mystery (MC 5, 21–22).

Ambrose of Milan completed his mystagogical preaching on baptism pointing toward the Eucharist when he said the following:

> You went there, you washed, you came to the altar, you began to
> see what you had not seen before: that is to say, through the font
> of the Lord and the preaching of the Lord's passion, at that moment
> your eyes were opened. ...
>   So, my beloved brothers, we have reached the altar, a subject of
> even greater richness (OS 3, 15).

Ambrose seemed convinced that the Eucharist is the pinnacle of the initiation experience. He spent the next three days preaching on its significance. He admonished his listeners to "understand how great a sacrament [the Eucharist] is" (OS 4, 26). He continued his encouragement the following day:

> You have come to the altar; the Lord Jesus calls you. ... Nothing
> could be sweeter (OS 5, 5).

> So you have come to the altar; you have received the body of Christ.
> Learn from another source the nature of the sacraments you have
> received. Listen to what blessed David says, ... "The Lord feeds me.
> I want for nothing. He has led me to a place of refreshment. ... You
> have prepared a meal for me. ... And your cup which inebriates,
> how glorious it is! (OS 5, 12–13).

> You have come to the altar, you have received the grace of Christ,
> you have taken the heavenly sacraments. The church rejoices in the
> redemption of so many, and is exultant with spiritual gladness
> (OS 5, 14).

The Eucharist was also the focus of the final two *Baptismal Homilies* of Theodore of Mopsuestia. Like his fellow mystagogues, he believed the Eucharist was central to the faith of those who had become Christian. As he began his fifth homily, Theodore said this:

Today ... I am contemplating to draw you, by the grace of God, to the nourishment of a bread, the nature of which you must know and the greatness of which you must learn with accuracy.

You will receive another food that cannot be described with words, and you will then be clearly fed by the grace of the Spirit whereby you will remain immortal in your bodies and immutable in your souls (BH 5, 71).

The testimony of recent neophytes also confirms the central role of the Eucharist in their lives. Unlike their predecessors in faith, contemporary neophytes have often experienced the celebration of the Eucharist many times. The secrecy of the *disciplina arcani* of the fourth century is no more, but the central role of the Eucharist in the ongoing life of faith for the neophytes and all the faithful remains.

Recent neophytes testified to their growing hunger for the Eucharist as the catechumenate progressed and their continuing hunger as they live out their faith. The Sunday Eucharist is the time at which they experience the presence of God in their lives, nourishing them in word and in sacrament. It is in the Sunday Eucharist that all the faithful are continually initiated into the saving mystery of Christ and sent forth to live the faith they have received.

Formed by the Word of God

All catechesis, throughout the initiation process, is rooted in the word of God. The analysis of the experience of recent neophytes concluded that "All involved in the process have a strong sense that God is revealed when the word of God is proclaimed and shared" (see conclusion 6 on page 70). The ancient mystagogues used Scriptures, interpreting the mysteries experienced in the sacraments through the use of allegory and typology (see conclusions 2 and 3 on page 92). The Scriptures are also central to the church's vision as expressed in the contemporary *Rite of Christian Initiation of Adults* (see conclusions 3 and 6 on page 106).

In the five parishes I visited, lectionary-based catechesis was central to catechetical sessions during the catechumenate.[15] The readings from the Sunday liturgy set the agenda for what would be discussed at meetings with catechists, sponsors, and catechumens.

The ancient mystagogues cited Scripture passages throughout their preaching. Often they proclaimed a passage before beginning their preaching. Even when preaching during Lent on the Lord's Prayer and the Creed, they cited the Scriptures over and over again. Their constant use of Scriptures in their preaching indicated their strong belief that God is revealed through the word.

The Rite, too, emphasizes the central role of the Scriptures in the initiation process:

> Suitable catechesis is ... solidly supported by celebrations of the word (RCIA 75.1).

> Celebrations of the word may also be held in connection with catechetical or instructional meetings of the catechumens, so that these will occur in a context of prayer (RCIA 84).

When describing the period of postbaptismal catechesis or mystagogy, the Rite points to the centrality of the word of God when it says the following:

> This is a time for the community and the neophytes together to grow in deepening their grasp of the paschal mystery and in making it part of their lives through meditation on the Gospel, sharing in the eucharist, and doing works of charity (RCIA 244).

> The neophytes are, as the term "mystagogy" suggests, introduced into a fuller and more effective understanding of mysteries through the Gospel message they have learned. ... For they have truly ... tasted more deeply the sweetness of God's words (RCIA 245).

The word of God provides the context within which all catechesis takes place. Engagement with the word of God is an essential element of the Christian life, from the beginning of the initiation process until that day all the faithful stand before the word enthroned on high. The Christian faithful are formed, both individually and as a community, by continually listening to the word of God and reflecting on its message.

Who Are the Significant People in an Authentically Mystagogical Initiation Process?

An effective initiation process is not an object to be examined. It is not a theory to be investigated. An effective initiation process is a gathering of people. It varies from day to day and place to place. It is more of a conglomeration of persons than a single entity. Reflecting on the various persons encountered and the words left behind by others involved in mystagogy, it seems that at least three important individuals or groups of people are involved in shaping an effective mystagogy:[16] the sponsors and godparents, the clergy in the local community, and the catechists.

Sponsors and Godparents

While the role of the sponsor is not discussed in much detail in the preaching of most of the late-fourth-century mystagogues, there is some evidence that they played a significant role in the writings of Hippolytus and Egeria and in the preaching of Theodore of Mopsuestia.

Hippolytus wrote about "those who come forward for the first time to hear the word" and the testimony required by "those who have brought them" (AT 15). "Those who have brought them" are again questioned and "bear witness … when those who are to receive baptism are chosen" (AT 20). Hippolytus seems to presume that "those who have brought them" know the candidates well enough to give appropriate testimony about their personal lives.

Egeria likewise testifies to the presence of godparents. She too describes how the bishop questions the godparents about the behavior of "those seeking baptism" (ET 45.2). At the daily morning gatherings during Lent, the godparents accompany "those to be baptized … while the bishop is teaching" (ET 46.1). With godparents at their sides, the catechumens recited the Creed during Holy Week. During Easter week, "any of the faithful who wish to hear the Mysteries" gather with the neophytes each day to hear the mystagogical preaching of the bishop. It is probably safe in presuming that the godparents would be among those faithful who gather with the neophytes.

When speaking about the enrollment of the one to be baptized in a

register—what we would today call the rite of election—Theodore of
Mopsuestia uses the analogy of the church as the city of God. As he
does so, he speaks of the role of the sponsor when he says the
following:

> This is the reason why, as if he were a stranger to the city and to
> its citizenship, a specially appointed person, who is from the city in
> which he is going to be enrolled and who is well versed in its mode
> of life, conducts him to the registrar and testifies for him to the
> effect that he is worthy of the city and of its citizenship and that, as
> he is not versed in the life of the city or in the knowledge of how to
> behave in it, he himself would be willing to act as guide to his
> inexperience.
>
> This rite is performed for those who are baptized by the person
> called godfather. ... [The godparent] only bears witness to what the
> catechumen has done and to the fact that he has prepared himself
> in the past to be worthy of the city and of its citizenship. He is
> justly called a sponsor because by his words [the catechumen] is
> deemed worthy to receive baptism. ...
>
> Your godfather who is in it is possessed of great diligence to
> teach you, who are a stranger and a newcomer to that great city,
> all the things that pertain to it and to its citizenship, so that you
> should be conversant with its life without any trouble and anxiety
> (BH 6, 25–26).

Theodore also mentions in later homilies the ways in which the
godparent participates in the ritual of baptism.[17] The role of the
sponsor is one of guide and initiator into life as a citizen of the city of
God. Not only does the sponsor witness to the church about the life of
the candidate, but the sponsor witnesses to the candidate about the
life of the church.

Today's Rite is even more explicit about the role and duties of the
sponsor and godparent:[18]

> A sponsor accompanies any candidate seeking admission as a
> catechumen. Sponsors are persons who have known and assisted
> the candidates and stand as witnesses to the candidates' moral
> character, faith, and intention. ...

Their godparents … accompany the candidates on the day of election, at the celebrations of the sacraments of initiation and during the period of mystagogy. Godparents are persons chosen by the candidates on the basis of example, good qualities, and friendship, delegated by the local Christian community, and approved by the priest. It is the responsibility of godparents to show the candidates how to practice the Gospel in personal and social life, to sustain the candidates in moments of hesitancy, to bear witness, and to guide the candidates' progress in the baptismal life. … They continue to be important during the time after reception of the sacraments when the neophytes need to be assisted so that they remain true to their baptismal promises (RCIA 10–11).

The witness of Hippolytus and Egeria and the preaching of the Theodore of Mopsuestia, along with what the Rite says about the role of the sponsor and godparent, affirms the conclusion from recent neophytes: Sponsors who witness their faith and offer concrete personal support to the catechumens and neophytes are a necessary component to an effective initiation experience.

Recent neophytes often expressed their gratitude for the ministry of the sponsors and godparents who accompanied them on the journey of conversion. They spoke of the encouragement and support they received not only from their sponsor's presence but also from the witness of their words and their lives. Several talked about how important their godparents and sponsors continue to be as they seek to live out the faith they have received. A simple greeting or a short conversation with one's sponsor at the weekly gathering for the Sunday Eucharist often gives added comfort and encouragement as the life of the neophyte becomes more routine. Within the small group gatherings during the initiation process and in individual conversation with sponsors and godparents, the candidates and neophytes are nourished and strengthened in their attempts to live out the faith day to day.

Ordained Pastoral Leaders in the Local Community

One of the primary roles of the local bishop in the fourth century is now often performed by priests in local communities. It is the role of pastoring. This is especially evident in the preaching of the fourth-century mystagogues. Today's pastors are called by the Rite to a similar role:

> Priests ... have the responsibility of attending to the pastoral and personal care of the catechumens, especially those who seem hesitant and discouraged (RCIA 13).

Recent neophytes reported that the pastoral care offered by priests was important to them as they journeyed through the initiation process. This pastoral care included preaching that focused on their faith journey, especially at the celebrations of the various rituals that are part of the Rite. It likewise included personal care of the catechumens which involved individual conversations and personal witness of their faith during the catechumenate and mystagogy. The willingness of priests to share their own faith struggles was viewed by neophytes as a positive element in helping them face the struggles they would encounter as Christians in the world today. Somehow knowing that persons in leadership in the church shared experiences of weakness made it possible for the candidates and neophytes to face their own weaknesses.

It was important to many of the neophytes that they had come to know those who pastored the community in some personal way. While this was often done in group settings, the mere presence of the clergy from the local community communicated a significance to the journey on which they had embarked.

It seems significant that all of the late-fourth-century mystagogues preached both catechetical and mystagogical sermons.[19] Their catechetical sermons generally focused on the Creed and the Lord's Prayer and were part of the immediate preparations during Lent of catechumens for initiation.[20] While their sermons would not generally be considered self-revealing, the enthusiasm for the faith proclaimed in their sermons does indicate some personal investment in the preaching task. Since the communities were small compared to dioceses today, it was likely that the bishop was as well known at the end of the fourth century as a pastor would be in an urban parish today. Some relationship seems to have existed between the catechumens and the bishop who would preside over the sacraments of initiation prior to the celebration. While they were not necessarily well known to each other, neither were the mystagogues strangers to the neophytes when they began their preaching.

While the period of postbaptismal catechesis or mystagogy lasts considerably longer today than it did during the late fourth century,[21] the presider and preacher at public gatherings of the neophytes and anyone else who might be interested remains a constant. Today the mystagogical preaching of the period of postbaptismal catechesis takes place during the Sunday Masses for the neophytes (RCIA 247). In that liturgical gathering of the local community, it is the ordained ministers of the local community who serve as primary mystagogues for the neophytes. Their preaching is the postbaptismal catechesis. Their relationship with the neophytes continues to influence them as they gather week after week throughout their lives, as they hear his preaching on a regular basis and experience his pastoral care as regular members of the parish.

The role of pastoral leadership is significant to the life of the parish and its parishioners. When that relationship begins during the initiation process and is experienced as personal, it seems to have a greater impact on the neophytes and on their continuing membership in the parish and the church.

The Rite also encourages the local bishop to celebrate the Eucharist with the neophytes of the diocese at least once during the year (RCIA 251). This would normally be the second time the neophytes would have heard their bishop preach—the first time being at the rite of election at the beginning of Lent (RCIA 118–137). These two encounters with the local bishop witness to the catechumens' and the neophytes' relationship with the larger church.

Catechists

In most parish communities, the catechists spend more time and energy than the sponsors, godparents, or ordained leaders in the ministry of initiation. They are often intimately involved in preparing for the various rituals, in discernment, in prayer, and in catechetical instruction. They often come to know the inquirers, catechumens, and neophytes quite well. They often see their own role as very significant in the faith formation of new Christians. However, the witness of the neophytes and the vision of the church do not support this claim.

The recent neophytes I interviewed rarely talked about their experience of catechesis as being significant in their faith formation. They sometimes talked about the relationships they developed with particular catechists, the witness of the catechist's faith, and the welcome they experienced through the ministry of the catechists. However, they rarely mentioned catechetical sessions or the input they received during catechetical sessions as being of any great significance. This may be due to the fact that the Christian initiation of adults is primarily a rite, and rites often have more power over us than words of instruction.

Hippolytus mentioned that there were "teachers" who gave instruction to the catechumens (AT 18), but he didn't say much more than that about their role. Some of the late-fourth-century mystagogues served as catechists while they were presbyters, but we only have records of what they preached and taught during the immediate preparations of Lent,[22] and the fact that they were either presbyters or bishops at the time indicates that their roles were significantly different from the role of teacher or catechist.

The Rite, too, has little to say about the role of catechists. The Rite does say this:

> Catechists, who have an important office for the progress of the catechumens and for the growth of the community, should, whenever possible, have an active part in the rites. When deputed by the bishop they may perform the minor exorcisms and blessings contained in the ritual. When they are teaching, catechists should see that their instruction is filled with the spirit of the Gospel, adapted to the liturgical signs and the cycle of the church's year, suited to the needs of the catechumens, and as far as possible enriched by local traditions (RCIA 16).

Catechists are reminded in several places about the content of their catechesis (see RCIA 38, 75, 78, 138–139). They are, however, not mentioned at all in the section on the period of postbaptismal catechesis or mystagogy, though someone clearly performs a leadership role in the "assemblies of the neophytes" mentioned in the *National Statutes*.[23]

Since catechists often spend more time with inquirers, catechumens, and neophytes than other ministers of initiation, their role is potentially significant. As a catechist and as a trainer of catechists, I have experienced God at work in the ministry of catechist. This is especially true when the catechist is focused on assisting the inquirers, catechumens, Elect, and neophytes in recognizing the presence of Christ in their own lives, in the word proclaimed, and in the rituals celebrated. When catechists, however, emphasize the content of their instructions, when they are concerned about "what the catechumens should know," then their ministry is often forgettable.

When catechists do their ministry well, they appear insignificant, because the word and ritual are permitted to shine brightly. However, when they do their ministry poorly, they are perceived as unimportant, because the content of the catechism is, in fact, rather insignificant when compared with the mystery of God's revealing power in life's experiences, in word, and in sacrament.

How Does the Tradition Affirm and Challenge Present Initiatory Practices?

The previous discussion both affirms and challenges the present practices of mystagogy in the United States. It affirms many of the conclusions from the previous chapters, offering challenges to the present practices of Christian initiation of adults in many parish communities. It offers two challenges in particular: to see the whole of Christian initiation as a mystagogical process and to recognize the real presence of Christ in all its various manifestations, especially in the word of God proclaimed.

Christian Initiation As a Mystagogical Process

The whole ritual and catechetical process that the church today calls the *Rite of Christian Initiation of Adults* is meant to be experienced as an integrated whole and a mystagogical process. We have examined the initiation process—and the period of postbaptismal catechesis or mystagogy in particular—from several different vantage points and have analyzed various parts of the process. We have discovered that all the ministries, all the various rituals, all the different stages are intimately related to one another. Each part of the process builds on the experiences of the previous stage(s). Each ritual presumes that the previous ritual was celebrated and celebrated well. The catechesis of each period is in many ways mystagogical. Mystagogy does not wait for the period of postbaptismal catechesis. It begins early in the process, or it is not effective.

The focus of this book has been mystagogy. In the beginning we were tempted by the current ritual book to limit our understanding of mystagogy to the period of postbaptismal catechesis. Yet we have found mystagogical practices in all the stages and rituals of the process. Unless all the stages are appropriately related to one another and mystagogical in nature, they will inevitably be ineffective. Unless the catechesis during all the stages and the many rituals celebrated throughout the process are connected to one another and to the liturgical year, it will be difficult at best for the whole sequence of events to be experienced as an integrated whole. If the various ministers do not share a common concern for the inquirers, the catechumens, the Elect, and neophytes, if their ministries are not coordinated with one another, the mystagogy of the Easter season and beyond cannot help the neophytes integrate their experiences and understandings into a life of faith that makes sense.

Each minister, each stage, each ritual is interrelated with all of the other ministers, stages, and rituals. The catechesis that is part of postbaptismal mystagogy builds on a foundation that has been laid during the previous stages. The old saying that a chain is as strong as its weakest link surely applies here. The period of postbaptismal catechesis cannot be effectively or authentically mystagogical if that dimension is lacking in previous periods. It cannot overcome rituals that were not celebrated well. It cannot make up for catechesis that is incomplete. It cannot lead to a deeper conversion if an initial conversion never took place.

All of initiation is an integrated process—a process that does not end with initiation or even with the first anniversary of initiation and the completion of the formal period of mystagogy. Many of the suggestions for developing an effective mystagogy mentioned in the next and final chapter will seem to have little to do with the period of postbaptismal catechesis and mystagogy. They will, however, be integral to its continued development. They will focus on the whole of the initiation process and beyond, for the Christian life is itself mystagogical when our experience of God in life, in word, and in ritual are seriously reflected on and intimately integrated one to another.

The Real Presence of Christ

The present practices in five parishes with effective mystagogies, the witness of the late fourth century, and the *Rite of Christian Initiation of Adults* affirm and challenge the whole church to take seriously the words proclaimed at the end of every reading from the sacred Scriptures—"The Word of the Lord." While we Catholic Christians profess with our lips that the word of God proclaimed is one of the epiphanies of the Lord—one of the several ways in which we can experience the real presence—our actions often don't seem to confirm that profession of faith. Without being fundamentalist, recent neophytes, ancient mystagogues, and the current Rite seriously proclaim that God speaks to people today through the word written long ago but very much alive in the world today.

An effective mystagogy—an authentically mystagogical initiation process—takes seriously this real presence. For much of the past several centuries, the Catholic Church's defense of the real presence in the Eucharist has not only overshadowed the real presence in the assembly gathered, in the ministers ministering, and in the word proclaimed, but it has almost totally eclipsed this ancient understanding of Christ's postresurrection presence in the world. The renewal of the church initiated at Vatican II has reestablished this focus on the multiple presences of Christ in the world today (see "Notes," Chapter 4, note 4). When those who preach the word of God, those who teach the faith, and those who celebrate together the rituals really believe that Christ is present in their midst, that witness itself opens the inquirers, catechumens, Elect, and neophytes to Christ's presence and to the possibility of real conversion. Unless one experiences the real presence of Christ in all its manifestations, it will be unlikely that one will experience an effective mystagogy or an authentic conversion to Christ.

The final chapter offers some suggestions for a contemporary mystagogical practice that sees the whole of the Christian life as mystagogical and recognizes the real presence of Christ in word and ritual and in assembly and ministers. As the search for an effective mystagogy comes to an end, these discoveries will guide us not only as mystagogues, but as the Christian faithful who have experienced God's grace at work in our lives.

Chapter 5

Suggestions for a Contemporary Mystagogical Practice

It is now time to make some practical suggestions for a contemporary mystagogical practice. This is the chapter many readers will look to first, ignoring the chapters that preceded it. It is my hope that if you are one of these readers you will go back to the beginning, because this entire book is meant to be an experience of mystagogy.

Mystagogy is not simply a period of time; it is a way of doing theology, a way of coming to understand the mystery of God. To borrow a sentence from the *Catechism of the Catholic Church*, one could say the following:

> [Mystagogy] aims to initiate people into the mystery of Christ by proceeding from the visible to the invisible, from the sign to the thing signified, from the "sacraments" to the "mysteries" (CCC 1075).[1]

A mystagogical method, as described in the introduction to this book, is as follows:

1. Mystagogy begins with reflection on experience. The mystagogue invites those who are present for this kind of catechesis to reflect on a specific event—to remember the sounds, sights, smells, tastes, and tactile experiences that were part of the event. They are also invited to remember the thoughts and feelings of that experience. They are encouraged not only to reflect on what they experienced but also on how

they experienced it. (The first and second chapters of this book were an attempt to look at some people's experience of mystagogy and to look at what was common in their experience.)

2. The mystagogue then shares part of the Christian story and vision. The Scriptures, the church's liturgy, history, traditions, and theology are all part of this story or vision. (In this book, both the witness of the late fourth century and the church's contemporary documents about mystagogy were that sharing of the Christian vision.)

3. All the participants enter into a conversation with their experience and the church's story and vision. (Chapter 4 sought to bring the experience of recent neophytes into dialogue with ancient mystagogues and the contemporary church documents.)

4. Finally, the mystagogue invites those gathered to ask themselves what they will do differently as a result of the insights gained during the conversation. (This chapter attempts to make some suggestions about future practices regarding mystagogy.)

Mystagogy does not just stop when people come to a new understanding of their encounter with mystery. It continues by asking these questions: "Now what? What are we to do as a result of our new understandings?" This chapter attempts to answer these questions about mystagogy itself.

Starting at the End: Be Clear about the Goals

When building a house, one does not start by digging a hole in the ground for the basement. While that will be an important early step in the process, the first step is to look at the end product. Complete architectural drawings are needed before the first shovelful of earth is moved. The architect, too, does not start with the basement or the foundation. One must be clear about what kind of house one wants even before the drawing begins.

When planning for an effective initiation process, the ministers of initiation need to be clear about the goals of Christian initiation. If the primary goal of initiation is getting people baptized, the Easter Vigil will be a kind of graduation. If the only goal of initiation is helping people have a strong personal relationship with Christ, one should not be surprised if neophytes cease to be members of the worshiping community shortly after completing their initiation. If the ultimate goal of initiation is to help people become Catholic Christians who participate in the liturgical life of the parish community, full, active, conscious participation in the Sunday liturgy is more likely to result. If the final goal of initiation is social consciousness, we are likely to see men and women who give of their time and talents to serve the needs of others.

Our conversation between recent neophytes, ancient mystagogues, and the current *Rite of Christian Initiation of Adults* demonstrated that the goal of Christian initiation is new behaviors and new relationship that enable the person to live the Christian life (see pages 112–120). If initiation, and mystagogy in particular, is to help people achieve these goals, all those involved must be clear about these goals from the very beginning.

New Behaviors

When planning for an effective initiation, one could justifiably ask, "What new behaviors are the results of an effective initiation process?" The Rite, when describing mystagogy, mentions three new behaviors as goals of initiation: "meditation on the Gospels, sharing in the eucharist and doing the works of charity" (RCIA 244). Looking back to the period of the catechumenate, the Rite looks for these same behaviors, calling catechumens to "turn more readily to God in prayer, to bear witness to the faith, in all things to keep their hopes set on Christ, to follow supernatural inspiration in their deeds, and to practice love of neighbor, even at the cost of self-renunciation" (RCIA 75.2).

The recent neophytes interviewed for this book mentioned specific behaviors that were a result of their conversion. These behaviors include being more patient, understanding, and forgiving with others and with themselves and spending more time in prayer and reflection on the scriptures. Some also included spending time doing charitable work beyond their own families and friends. Some added participation in some ministry of the parish. The preaching of the ancient mystagogues also encouraged the neophytes and the faithful to practice Gospel charity, to participate in the liturgical life of the church.

One, therefore, could justifiably say that the new behaviors that are the goal of Christian initiation are directed toward Gospel charity—love of God and love of neighbor. These are also manifested both in public behaviors—such as participation in the liturgical life of the church and engagement in works of charity—and private behaviors—such as spending time in personal prayer and reflection on the Gospels. They are both personal and communal.

New Relationships

One could also ask, "What new relationships ought to result from an effective initiation experience?" Like the new behaviors mentioned above, these new relationships are both personal and communal. The newly initiated ought to have new or deeper relationships with God, with the church, and with the all of creation. These new relationships will likely include new friendships within the catechumenal and parish communities. They might also include a deepening relationship of understanding, compassion, and reconciliation within relationships that already exist. Old animosities might be overcome by a new willingness to forgive and understand others who may have hurt or been hurt in the past by the new Christian.

Christian faith is more than an intellectual assent, and it affects more than one's close personal relationships. It is also a relationship with God—Father, Son, and Holy Spirit. Through faith, one enters an intimate relationship with God. Ancient mystagogues and recent neophytes alike testify to this growing relationship between believer and God. This relationship is often described as a relationship of love—a love that is always open to discovering more about oneself and about the beloved. This relationship is not merely a personal relationship with one's Lord and savior. It is not simply personal. It has a communal dimension as well, for God is encountered not only in the deep recesses of the heart but also in the community of faith and in all that God has created.

A growing sense of belonging and a concern for the church are also aspects of the new relationships that develop as part of the experience of Christian conversion.[2] A sense of belonging to something both bigger than oneself and even bigger than the local parish is developed through the experiences of God at work in the rituals of the RCIA.[3]

New and deepening relationships with God, with individual persons and with the church are meant to be part of the conversion that takes place as part of the initiation process.

Living the Christian Life

These new behaviors and new relationships demonstrate in very real ways how the new Christian is living the Christian life. While no one in the church ever perfectly lives Christian charity, it is certainly one of the goals we are all challenged to strive for. As such, it is—and ought to be—one of the goals of every initiation process. It ought to motivate how ministers of initiation evangelize, catechize, and celebrate the mysteries of God's action in our lives. Once clear about the goals of Christian initiation, one can begin to look at how one implements the Rite.

Back to the Beginning: Mystagogical Throughout

Mystagogy ought to be part of the entire initiation process. If one waits until after Easter to begin, it will be too late. Unless the entire initiation process is mystagogical, mystagogy will be ineffective, and it will be difficult—if not impossible—to help those coming to the Christian faith achieve the goals of initiation.

Mystagogy always begins[4] with experience.[5] It takes people's experiences seriously. It reverences persons and their experiences of God. It helps people reflect on and find meaning in their experiences of the presence of God in their midst. Mystagogical catechesis presumes that God is always at work in the lives of God's people, whether realized or not. Mystagogy helps us break open our own experiences so that we can begin to recognize the many ways we have already encountered the Divine. It seeks opportunities for the mystery already encountered to dialogue with the mystery revealed in word and ritual. Mystagogical catechesis always asks at least three questions:[6]

1. What did you experience?

2. What does it mean?

3. What are you going to do about it?

These questions are always asked within a community. They are asked with a double meaning—"What did you personally experience?" and "What did you as a community experience?" The experience, meaning, and response are always both individual and communal.

The first question examines the whole experience, the senses, the intellect, the emotions, and the spirit. It might include questions such as, "What did you hear, see, feel, taste, smell, or sense? What thoughts, ideas, or memories came to mind? What emotions did you feel? What graces, temptations, and blessings did you experience? How was God a part of this experience?" As each individual answers these questions, the experience of the community will begin to be articulated, and the community's sense of the experience will emerge from the dialogue. There are no right or wrong answers to these questions. Each person's experience is valued. Different people will have experienced the same event in different ways. The catechists must be open to this reality and must not seek to dictate how others experience a particular event.

The second question looks at meaning within the context of faith. It asks and may offer answers to questions such as, "How does your experience relate to the experience of others in this community and in the larger Christian community, both now and throughout the tradition? To the sacred Scriptures? To the lives of others who have believed in God? To events in the history of the church? To the church's teachings?" It is obvious that the catechists will need to be familiar with the Christian Scriptures and tradition to help the candidates relate their experiences to this tradition.

The third question is future oriented. It seeks a response. It does not point to any specific response, but it does point in a particular direction—toward the life of faith. It simply asks, "How have you been affirmed or challenged? What are you going to do differently because of what you have learned about yourself, the church, God, Christ, and the Spirit, and so on?" It is meant to move the candidates beyond knowledge. It is meant to lead to conversion that is more than new information or new understanding. It is meant to lead to a conversion that is effective—that is, has concrete effects in people's lives including new behaviors and relationships. It is focused on living the Christian life, both individually and in community.

These same questions are asked throughout the initiation process. The experiences that are reflected on may differ during the various stages or periods of the Christian initiation of adults, but the process is similar.

A Mystagogical Precatechumenate

The *Rite of Christian Initiation of Adults* describes the period of evangelization or precatechumenate as "a time of evangelization"—a time when "the living God" and "Jesus Christ whom [God] has sent for the salvation of all" is "faithfully and constantly … proclaimed" (RCIA 36).

The whole period of the precatechumenate is set aside for this evangelization, so that the genuine will to follow Christ and seek baptism may mature (RCIA 37).

This initial evangelization is mystagogical when it takes seriously the real life experiences of the candidates, when it presumes that candidates come to the church having already experienced the grace of God in their lives.

The catechists help the candidates to look back at their own experiences and recognize God at work there. They help the candidates focus on how God is and has been active throughout their lives. They might ask candidates to remember a time when they experienced love or forgiveness, mercy or kindness, compassion or awe. They might share some of their own experiences as well—witnessing to the presence of Christ in their own lives.

Then they assist the candidates in relating their experience to the Christian tradition—to the great stories of our faith found in sacred Scripture—and to the lives of other believers throughout history. Finally, the catechists help the candidates identify the affirmations and challenges to their ways of living that are offered by these new insights. Joseph P. Sinwell and others offer many suggestions for how this might be done.[7]

The catechist might also present opportunities for candidates to experience God in their lives. This might be through various forms of prayer or apostolic activity. Donald Neumann suggests that a catechist might take a group of candidates to a soup kitchen, a homeless shelter, or a prison for a couple of hours one week, and then lead them through a reflection on what they experienced during the following weeks.[8] The catechists might ask the candidates to describe their experiences at the soup kitchen, for instance. Then they might talk about the Gospel imperative offered in such stories as the parable of the final judgment (see Mt 35:31–46) or the second of the two great commandments (see Mk 12:31–33 or Mt 22:39). They might make reference to Conciliar documents such as the *Decree of the Apostolate of Lay People*, *Pastoral Constitution on the Church in the Modern World*, Paul VI's encyclical *Evangelization in the Modern World*, or some of the relevant sections of the *Catechism of the Catholic Church*.[9] Finally, the catechist asks the candidates to reflect on how their experiences among the poor and the teachings of Jesus and the church affirm and challenge the way in which they are currently living. The catechists allow the Gospel message to offer its own affirmations and challenges. They likewise admit that the Gospel mandate is not always followed perfectly, but that the challenge of the Gospel calls us to conversion over and over again as we seek to live the Christian faith more perfectly throughout our lives.

A period of evangelization that is mystagogical begins with personal experience, which is related to the Gospel and the church's tradition as well as to the experience of others who journey with them, and leads the candidates into new insights about God, the church, and themselves. They encounter the mystery in their lives and begin to make connections between their faith, the faith of the church, and their everyday lives. This can lead to the

> initial conversion and intention to change their lives and to enter into a relationship with God in Christ ... the first stirrings of repentance, a start to the practice of calling upon God in prayer, a sense of the church and some experience of the company and spirit of Christians

of which the Rite speaks (RCIA 42).

A Mystagogical Catechumenate

A mystagogical catechumenate begins with reflection on the experience of the rite of acceptance into the order of catechumens. This reflection follows the same three questions that are part of every mystagogical reflection, questions about experience, meaning, and response.

The catechists asks the new catechumens questions about their experience—questions such as the following:

- What did you experience as the assembly gathered around you?

- What did you experience as the presider asked you, "What do you ask of God's church?"

- What were you thinking? Feeling?

- What memories or hopes came to mind?

- What was your experience as the cross was traced on your forehead, ears, eyes, lips, heart, shoulders, hands, and feet?

- What words or actions stand out in your memory of that experience?

Many other questions might be asked that help the catechumens reflect on the experience of becoming catechumens. Again, these questions are addressed in both the singular and plural forms, to both individual catechumens and the community of catechumens, sponsors, and catechists gathered together.

Depending on the answers that the catechumens give to these questions, the catechist might make connections to the church's understanding of Christ's real presence in the assembly gathered, in the ministers ministering, in the word proclaimed, and in the rituals performed. The catechist might relate the experience of being signed with the cross to the Gospel admonition that to be a disciple one must "take up the cross" (Mt 10:38, 16:24; Mk 8:34; Lk 9:23, 14:27). The presentation of a Bible might be related to Paul's statement, "I handed on to you as of first importance what I also received" (1 Cor 15:3). There are many other connections that could be made between the experience and the church's tradition.

Finally the catechist might ask the new catechumens, "What challenges does this new status in the church offer? What difference does it make that you are now a catechumen?"

These kinds of questions about this first ritual experience as a catechumen will be repeated after each of the rituals of catechumenate and the initiation process. They will be asked to reflect on their experience of the rite of election, the scrutinies, the presentations, and the sacraments of initiation.[10] In many ways, this is classic mystagogy—reflection on the experience of the mysteries, of the rituals, and sacramental action of the church. This kind of mystagogical catechesis is often called ritual or liturgical catechesis.

While the rite of acceptance is celebrated only once, celebrations of the word take place throughout the catechumenate. Over and over again, the Rite reminds its readers of the central place of celebrations of the word.[11]

> Among the rites belonging to the period of the catechumenate, then, celebrations of the word of God are foremost (RCIA 79).

During these celebrations of the word of God, especially when catechumens gather with the rest of the parish community on Sundays to form the assembly for the Liturgy of the Word, the preaching ought to be mystagogical. The bishops gathered at Vatican II described the role of preaching as

> proclamation of God's wonderful works in the history of salvation, that is, the mystery of Christ, which is ever-made present and active within us (CSL 35.2).

In a way, they describe all liturgical preaching as mystagogical. To be honest, we must admit that at the beginning of the third millennium of Christianity, all preaching does not seem to meet this criterion.

When the bishops of the United States described the preacher's task, they used terms that are familiar to the mystagogue:

> What [the preacher's] words can do is help people make connections between the realities of their lives and the realities of the Gospel. [They] can help them see how God in Jesus Christ has entered and identified himself with the human realities of pain and of happiness.
>
> In order to make such connections between the lives of the people and the Gospel, preacher[s] will have to be listener[s] before [they are] speaker[s].... [They] listen to the Scriptures, [they] listen to the people and [they] ask, "What are they saying to one another? What are they asking of one another?" And out of that dialogue between the Word of God in the Scriptures and the Word of God in the lives of [God's] people, the Word of God in preaching begins to take shape (FIYH 19–20).

The mystagogical categories of experience, meaning, and response—found in our three mystagogical questions—are integral to the preaching task:

> Without ultimate meaning, we are ultimately unsatisfied. If we are able to hear a word which gives our lives another level of meaning, which interprets them in relation to God, then our response is to turn to this source of meaning in an attitude of praise and thanksgiving (FIYH 13).

Liturgical homilies that assist the assembly in hearing the message of God, in grasping new understandings, and in responding to God's message are by their very nature mystagogical. They help catechumens, like effective catechesis,

> to turn more readily to God in prayer, to bear witness to the faith, in all things to keep their hopes set on Christ, to follow supernatural inspiration in their deeds, and to practice the love of neighbor, even at the cost of self-renunciation (RCIA 75.2).

When preachers preach mystagogical homilies, they not only help the catechumens, they also support the ongoing faith development of the whole assembly.

Catechumens are generally dismissed from the Sunday assembly immediately following the Liturgy of the Word. The Rite states the following:

> After the dismissal formulary, the group of catechumens goes out but does not disperse. With the help of some of the faithful, the catechumens remain together to share their joy and spiritual experiences (RCIA 67A).

The catechumens and one or more catechists "share their joy and spiritual experience" in what is sometimes called dismissal catechesis. This catechesis begins with the presumption that God is really present in the word proclaimed—that the Liturgy of the Word is an experience of God's revelation to God's people.[12] This is a significant presumption. It is at the heart of both the liturgical and catechetical renewal that resulted from Vatican II. It also seems to be one of the convictions of the Council that is often under-appreciated or unrecognized by many within the church.

Dismissal catechesis is mystagogical in that it reflects back on the experience of God revealing Godself during the Liturgy of the Word just celebrated and asks the three mystagogical questions:

1. What did you experience?

2. What does it mean?

3. What are you going to do about it?

The catechumens are invited to listen again to the word they heard proclaimed in the Liturgy of the Word. The catechist, or one of the catechumens, proclaims the Gospel (or one of the other lectionary readings) so that the catechumens might hear it again. They are asked to listen carefully for a word or phrase that speaks to their hearts, a word or phrase that challenges or affirms their faith. They are asked to listen again for God's voice calling to them. The emphasis is on hearing. "What did you hear?" is the central question. Each of the catechumens is asked to share the word or phrase they heard, the word of phrase that spoke to their heart, mind, spirit, or soul.

Often the catechumens are asked to listen to the reading again. During this second reading of the Scripture, they are asked to listen for an affirmation or challenge to their faith, to their attitudes, thoughts, behaviors, or relationships. They are, in a sense, asked, "What is the meaning of this Scripture passage for you today?" The question might also be phrased, "What is the message of God for you in this Scripture passage?"[13] Once again the catechumens are asked to share their answers with one another, aware that each person hears the message from their own experience and that God may be speaking to different people in different ways at the same time.

Once this sharing is completed, the catechumens are asked to reflect on their response to the reading. "What concrete action are you going to take in response to what you have heard?" might be the question. Since the answer to this question is sometimes deeply personal, the catechumens are often free to share or not to share their answers.

Finally, catechumens are asked to offer a prayer for one another. This might be a very specific request that God bless a particular catechumen with the grace needed to respond to that day's reading based on what was shared in the discussion that took place.

Ritual and dismissal catecheses are not the only types of catecheses that take place during the catechumenate. They are rather narrowly focused and limited, especially since dismissal catechesis usually takes place while the rest of the assembly celebrates the Liturgy of the Eucharist. Additional opportunities for catechesis during which the sponsors and other catechists participate also take place.

These, too, might be somewhat mystagogical in that the topic for the catechetical session grows out of the experience of the Sunday Liturgy of the Word.

When doing dismissal catechesis, one must avoid any notion of fundamentalism. While the church proclaims that the word is alive and that God speaks to God's people through the word, the church has also taught that the tools of contemporary Scripture scholarship should be used when one interprets these sacred writings. While the tools of modern scholarship are not explicitly used during dismissal catechesis, they might more explicitly influence the presentations and discussions that are a part of other catechetical sessions that take place during the catechumenate.

One of the most overlooked aspects of the catechumenate is the call of the Rite to be involved in the church's apostolic life.[14] This might include group activities in which all the catechumens and their sponsors participate in a particular apostolic activity, or it might include individual activities in which individual catechumens and sponsors engage in a variety of apostolic activities.[15] These might be one-time experiences or ongoing ministries in which the catechumens are involved. In any case, opportunities for mystagogical reflection on the experience of apostolic activity ought to be part of the catechumenate. Once again, the three mystagogical questions would be asked. The catechumens would be asked to reflect on their experience and to share that experience with other catechumens. The catechist(s) would assist them in reflecting on how God was present in that activity, using the Scriptures, traditions, and teaching of the church to help the catechumens connect their experience to the larger experience of the Christian community throughout history.[16] Finally, they would be asked to name the challenge God is placing before them as a result of their experience.

A Mystagogical Period of Purification and Enlightenment

During the period of purification and enlightenment, there are at least four opportunities for the Elect and their godparents to reflect with the catechists on the experience of God encountered in the rituals of the church. These include the rite of election and the three scrutinies. They might also include the optional sending of catechumens for election, the presentations of the Creed and the Lord's Prayer (if they have not already taken place), and the preparation rites on Holy Saturday. Like the process described above to reflect on the experience of the rite of acceptance into the order of catechumens (see pages 147–148), this takes place sometime after the celebration of the ritual.

Following the pattern established by some of the fourth-century mystagogues, sessions in preparation for some of the rituals might also take place. Just as they prepared the candidates for the celebrations of baptism and chrismation, so today's catechists might help prepare the catechumens for the various rites that are part of this period. These are not meant to be rehearsals for the rituals, but rather experiences that open the catechumens to the action of God in their lives through the rituals about to be celebrated.[17]

Hinman Powell and Sinwell provide a model for such preparations in *Ninety Days*.[18] Other models are also available.[19] These models are mystagogical in that they seek to relate the life experiences of the Elect and their godparents to the Scriptures and rituals of the church. While they do not explicitly ask the three mystagogical questions, they seek to lead the Elect toward a ritual experience of God's real presence in their lives.

The liturgical presider and preacher play significant roles during the period of purification and enlightenment. The various rituals—beginning with the sending of catechumens for election through the celebrations of election, the scrutinies, and presentations, to the preparation rites of Holy Saturday—all point to the importance of baptism in the experience of Lent, even for those who are already fully initiated.[20] Mystagogical preaching that helps the Elect and the whole assembly recognize the connections between the Lenten Gospels and the conversion called for by these seasons of baptism and reconciliation are essential to an effective period of purification and enlightenment.

A Mystagogical Period of Postbaptismal Catechesis

It seems redundant to speak of a mystagogical mystagogy. Though the period of postbaptismal catechesis and mystagogy was the original focus of this book, it has moved well beyond that scope. Now we come to the place where our search originally intended to go.

The Rite uses the terms period of postbaptismal catechesis and mystagogy as synonyms. As we have seen through our search for an effective mystagogy, they are not always the same. Waiting until the period of postbaptismal catechesis to begin mystagogy will always be too late. All of the mystagogical processes at work in the earlier periods of the Christian initiation of adults are at work in this period.

The period begins with the celebration of the sacraments of initiation, usually at the Easter Vigil. Like earlier rites, this ritual deserves to be reflected on mystagogically. The neophytes, their sponsors and godparents, and the entire assembly are invited to gather together during Easter week to ask themselves our three mystagogical questions:

1. What did you experience?

2. What does it mean?

3. What are you going to do about it?

The celebration of the Easter Vigil is so full of symbolism that it will probably take several gatherings to reflect on the whole experience. Several resources are available that may help with this process.[21] They all begin with the neophytes, sponsors, godparents, catechists, and other members of the local community gathering together during Easter week to begin the reflection of postbaptismal catechesis.

The neophytes, sponsors, godparents, catechists, and other members of the local community generally gather in the place where the rituals actually took place so that all the senses are engaged in the remembering of that event. The catechist who functions as chief mystagogue for such a session helps those gathered remember what happened by reminding them of the various ritual elements. The mystagogue might say something like this:

> We gathered in darkness around a fire, which we blessed. The Easter candle was blessed and lit from that fire. As we entered the assembly, the one carrying the Easter candle proclaimed, "Christ

our light" three times as the flame was passed throughout the community. Only the Elect were without candles. And when the whole church was filled with the light from that one flame, the Easter Proclamation was sung. What did you experience? What did you hear, feel, and sense as we celebrated the ritual of light at the beginning of the Vigil?

The mystagogue might then remind them that after the baptism, the neophytes were presented with candles, and that the whole assembly held burning candles as they renewed their baptismal promises. Once again the mystagogue would ask those who are gathered, "What did you experience? What did you hear, feel, sense as you held the candles after your baptism or as you renewed your baptismal promises?" After having an opportunity to share their experiences, the mystagogue might point out some of the Scripture passages that refer to light, passages such as the following:

In the beginning, when God created the heavens and the earth, the earth was a formless wasteland, and darkness covered the abyss, while a mighty wind swept over the waters.

Then God said, "Let there be light," and there was light. God saw how good the light was. God then separated the light from the darkness. God called the light "day," and the darkness he called "night." Thus evening came, and morning followed—the first day (Gn 1:1–5).

The LORD is my light and my salvation; / whom should I fear? (Ps 27:1).

"You are the light of the world. ... Your light must shine before others, that they may see your good deeds and glorify your heavenly Father" (Mt 5:14–16).

"I am the light of the world. Whoever follows me will not walk in darkness, but will have the light of life" (Jn 8:12).

"While you have the light, believe in the light, so that you may become children of the light" (Jn 12:36).

Let us then throw off the works of darkness [and] put on the armor of light (Rom 13:12).

Like the ancient mystagogues, the contemporary mystagogue seeks to help the neophytes and the rest of the faithful make connections between their lives—both individually and as a community—their experiences, the ritual experience of the Easter Vigil, and the sacred Scriptures. Several resources offer further suggestions for using the preaching of the ancient mystagogues in this postbaptismal reflection.[22]

In the fourth century, the mystagogue often pointed out the appropriate response of a new Christian to the new insights about the experience of baptism, anointing, and Eucharist. Today, the mystagogue might engage those gathered in this activity, asking them what they believe—based on all they have learned through their conversion experience—would be appropriate behavioral responses to what God has done in them. At the same time, the mystagogue and some of those who minister in the local community might share some of the ways the faithful have and do respond to their baptismal experience.

This same process is used over and over again as the mystagogues lead those gathered through a mystagogical reflection on the entire Easter Vigil.

While these postbaptismal catechetical sessions are an important part of the final stage of the Christian initiation of adults, most of what happens during this period takes place at the Sunday Eucharist. As the Rite itself reminds us,

> Since the distinctive spirit and power of the period of postbaptismal catechesis or mystagogy derive from the new, personal experience of the sacraments and of the community, its main setting is the so-called Masses for neophytes, that is, the Sunday Masses of the Easter season (RCIA 247).

> All the neophytes and their godparents should make an effort to take part in the Masses for the neophytes and the entire local community should be invited to participate in them. Special places in the congregation are to be reserved for the neophytes and their

godparents. The homily and, as circumstances suggest, the general intercessions should take into account the presence and needs of the neophytes (RCIA 248).

The Rite implies that all of the preaching at the Sunday Masses of the Easter season should focus on the fact that neophytes are present in the midst of the community. All of the homilies of the Easter season should be mystagogical, helping the neophytes make connections between their new experience of the sacraments, their new experience of being members of the Christian community, the Gospels of the Easter season, and their everyday lives.[23]

Opportunities for "doing the works of charity" should also be provided for the neophytes.[24] This should not, however, be the first time the neophytes are introduced to the ministries of service practiced in the local community. As indicated above and in the section "A Mystagogical Precatechumenate," especially page 146, experiences among the poor should take place from the very beginning of the initiation process. Opportunities for further reflection on these apostolic activities should also be part of the period of postbaptismal catechesis.[25] While many neophytes may be interested in performing liturgical ministries such as lectors or extraordinary ministers of the Eucharist, ministry among the poor and needy should continue to be part of the neophytes' first year as fully initiated members of the Christian faithful.[26]

Ministers of Initiation: Mystagogues All

Since mystagogical processes are at work throughout the initiation process, those involved in the ministry of initiation are, in a sense, all mystagogues. From the catechists who first help the candidates reflect on the presence of God in their past experiences to the preachers who proclaim the saving action of God in word and sacrament during the period of postbaptismal catechesis, all share a mystagogical ministry. Whether explicitly or implicitly, they all seek to help the candidates, catechumens, Elect, and neophytes in their own ways to answer the mystagogical questions. They all seek to help them make connections between their own life experiences and the word, rituals, traditions, and ministries of the church. Even if they only walk directly with the candidates during inquiry or with the catechumens during the catechumenate, they serve as initial mystagogues, opening the way of faith before those who are on the initiation journey.

Mystagogical ministers always recognize that conversion is the work of God, that they are God's servants, and that God dwells in all people. They are often in awe of the power of God, which they are privileged to witness and participate in as they walk with men and women of faith along the journey of Christian initiation.

Mystagogical Communities

When the Rite describes the ministries and offices that are part of the Christian initiation of adults, it begins with the people of God—the local community of the faithful.[27] In many instances, it was the witness of the local community that inspired the neophytes to begin the initiation process. Mystagogical communities are places in which people recognize and cherish the real presence of Christ in the community gathered, in the word proclaimed, in the rituals celebrated, in the ministers serving. The reality of Christ present in their midst and in one another is both proclaimed and experienced even by visitors.[28]

Mystagogical communities are places in which people recognize the connection between liturgy and life, between what happens in church on Sunday morning and what happens throughout the community throughout the week. Mystagogical communities are also places in which adults are encouraged to reflect on and share their faith with one another through small basic communities, faith-sharing groups, and other adult formation programs. This creates a place where people expect to reflect on their experiences of God, on the meaning of those experiences, and on the appropriate Christian response to those experiences of God present in their midst.

Mystagogical communities are places in which all the faithful are invited to participate in the Christian initiation process, actively participating in the liturgy. They are communities in which catechumens experience the church's welcome during the various celebrations during the initiation process. During the period of purification and enlightenment and the period of postbaptismal catechesis, members of the community gather with the Elect and the neophytes to reflect on the meaning of their baptismal call and their experience of God through the celebrations of the sacraments of initiation. Just as they did during the late fourth century, the faithful join in the catechetical gatherings that are part of the initiation process.

Mystagogical communities are also places where apostolic ministry and concern for the poor and the needy are part of the community's everyday life. When a parish community actively encourages many different apostolic activities, this creates an environment in which catechumens and neophytes alike recognize that service to the poor is indeed a constitutive element of the Christian faith, where practicing "love of neighbor, even at the cost of self-renunciation" (RCIA 75.2) is not unusual, and where "doing the works of charity" (RCIA 244) is not something new to neophytes.

Mystagogical Preachers and Presiders

The Christian initiation of adults is first and foremost a ritual process.[29] As such, the presider and preacher play major roles in the initiation process. Mystagogical presiders recognize the real presence of Christ in the assemblies and the rituals over which they preside. When they lead an assembly in prayer, they are likewise aware that Christ is at work in and through them. Using gestures and voice, the words of the rituals as well as their own words, they become instruments of God's grace. They are familiar with the rites, with their histories and development. They know how to appropriately adapt the rituals to particular individuals and communities with whom they minister. They recognize and at times are in awe of the power God demonstrates through the rites over which they preside. They are not afraid to be lavish with the symbols and grand with their gestures.

Mystagogical preachers know that God continues to be revealed through the word proclaimed. Throughout the previous section of this chapter, the preacher was described as a significant person in a mystagogical catechumenate (see pages 148–150), a mystagogical period of purification and enlightenment (see pages 152–153), and a mystagogical period of postbaptismal catechesis (see pages 153–157). The fourth-century mystagogues sought to answer the three mystagogical questions in their homilies. Today's preachers should also guide the assembly as it reflects on the Scriptures, helping it to recognize God's message for this community at this time.[30] At times their answers to the mystagogical questions will be more direct than at others. But they will always seek to communicate God's message to God's people, helping them make connections between the word proclaimed and their lives as the Christian faithful.

All preachers and presiders are human vessels God uses to communicate to God's people. Each has both strengths and weaknesses. Each will use those gifts according to their abilities. Many presiders and preachers today have not had much training or practice with the *Rite of Christian Initiation of Adults* nor with the language or experience of conversion that underlies these rites. Few seminaries or schools of theology adequately prepare ordained ministers for presiding and preaching at these rituals, and most priests today were educated prior to the development of these rituals and thus received no formal education concerning these rites or this process of initiation.[31] As these rites are celebrated again and again, and as preachers and presiders experience the power of these rites themselves and hear the witness of those who have experienced their power, their ability to preside and preach is likely to improve.[32]

Mystagogical Catechists

The Rite itself has little to say about the role of catechists.[33] In most parish communities, however, the catechists primarily provide the leadership in the implementation of the Rite. Mystagogical catechists know the difference between formation and education, between catechesis and indoctrination (see "Notes," Introduction, note 24). They know that the initiation process is concerned with more than learning *about* God and the church. Mystagogical catechists seek to help candidates, catechumens, the Elect, and neophytes grow in their relationships with God and their fellow believers who make up the church.

Mystagogical catechists lead the candidates as they reflect on their experiences of God at work in their lives, in their experiences of prayer, of hearing God's word, and of apostolic activity (see the section "A Mystagogical Precatechumenate," pages 145–147). They help the catechumens recognize how God has worked through the rites of the catechumenate and in their experiences of apostolic activities. They are also dismissal ministers who trust the catechumens to recognize the voice of God in the Liturgy of the Word from which they have been dismissed. Sometimes they are presiders at celebrations of the word, the minor exorcisms, or blessings of catechumens (RCIA 81–97). Mystagogical catechists help prepare catechumens and the Elect for the various rituals that take place during the process as well as reflect mystagogically on the experiences of the rites once they have been celebrated.

Mystagogical catechists always remember that the initiation process is about developing faith rather than learning religion, that it is about a deepening relationship with God and God's people, and that it is ultimately the work of God. They know that they teach as much by how they speak as the words that are spoken, by what they do as by what they say. They see themselves more as witnesses to God's presence in the world than as teachers who pass on the content of the faith. They know that both are important, but that a living faith is more significant than simply knowing the doctrine of the church. They know that doctrine serves faith, but is not itself faith.

Mystagogical catechists are always focused on building up the Christian community—the assembly of the faithful—as they strive to be the reign of God in the world today.

Mystagogical Sponsors and Godparents

Mystagogical sponsors and godparents walk with those they are sponsoring, sharing their faith as fellow questioners. They recognize that God is at work in the initiation process, in the people they are sponsoring, and in themselves. They recognize that God is really present in the assembly gathered, the word proclaimed, the rituals celebrated, and the ministers serving. They are not afraid to walk along the path of faith, though they are sometimes uncertain where it will lead.

Mystagogical godparents realize that though their ministry begins at the rite of election, it does not end with the celebration of the sacrament of initiation. They know that their relationship is ongoing, that they walk with their godchildren for the rest of their lives. They know that the questions will not end with the completion of the initiation process, but that the mystagogical questions will be asked and answered again and again throughout the life of every Christian. Mystagogical godparents are willing to live with the questions whose answers are often incomplete and sometimes mysterious. They are willing to walk with themselves and their godchildren through the ambiguities of lives that seek to be faithful to the God who has called them both.

The Search Continues

The search for an effective mystagogy never ends. It goes on and on. It is the search itself, the search for the mystery that is the living God that is mystagogy. If we think we have found it, it will elude us all the more. An effective mystagogy is an authentic initiation process, a process that does not end with baptism, confirmation, and the first sharing at the eucharistic table. It is a process that continues throughout one's life, as one gathers with other believers, listens to the living word in an ever-changing world, shares the bread of life and the cup of salvation anew, and witnesses to God's ever-present actions in the world.

An effective mystagogy is a lifelong endeavor to recognize the real presence of Christ in all of life's experiences. It is an attempt to answer again and again the mystagogical questions:

1. What did you experience?

2. What does it mean?

3. What are you going to do about it?

With each new experience, with each new revelation of God's presence in our lives and in our world, the questions will be asked again and again. As we seek to answer them in each new context, we will experience an effective mystagogy.

The search for an effective mystagogy will only end when we stand before the Lamb once slain who lives forever. Then, face-to-face with the living God, our questions shall all pass away and we shall know God as surely as we are known (see 1 Cor 13:12). Until then, let the search continue.

Appendix 1

Excerpts from *Rite of Christian Initiation of Adults: Provisional Text Approved for Interim Use in the Dioceses of the United States of America by the Bishops Committee on the Liturgy and the Executive Committee of the National Conference of Catholic Bishops and Confirmed by the Apostolic See (1974)*

Introduction

37. After this last stage has been completed, the community and the neophytes move forward together, meditating on the Gospel, sharing in the eucharist, and performing works of charity. In this way they understand the paschal mystery more fully and bring it into their lives more and more. The period of postbaptismal catechesis or mystagogia is the final period of initiation of the newly baptized.

38. A fuller, more fruitful understanding of the "mysteries" is acquired by the newness of the account given to the neophytes and especially by their experience of receiving the sacraments. They have been renewed in mind, have tasted more intimately the good word of God, have shared in the Holy Spirit, and have come to discover the goodness of the Lord. From this experience, which is proper to the Christian and is increased by the way he lives, they draw a new sense of the faith, the church, and the world.

39. This new frequenting of the sacraments enlightens the neophytes' understanding of the holy Scriptures and also increases their knowledge of men [sic] and develops the experience in the community itself. As a result, the relationship of the neophyte with the rest of the faithful becomes easier and more beneficial. The time of postbaptismal catechesis is of great importance so that the neophytes,

helped by their sponsors, may enter into a closer relationship with the faithful and bring them renewed vision and a new impetus.

40. Since the nature and force proper to this period came from the new, personal experience of the sacraments and of the community, the main place for the postbaptismal catechesis or mystagogia will be the Masses for the neophytes, that is, the Sunday Masses of the Easter season. In these celebrations, besides meeting with the community and sharing in the mysteries, the newly baptized will find the readings of the Lectionary appropriate for them, especially the readings of Year A. For this reason, the whole local community should be invited to these Masses along with the neophytes and their sponsors. The texts for the Masses may be used even when the initiation is celebrated outside the usual time.

57. The Masses for neophytes are celebrated on all the Sundays after the First Sunday of Easter. The community, the newly baptized and their godparents are urgently invited to participate (see no. 40).

The Period of Postbaptismal Catechesis or Mystagogia

235. To strengthen the first steps of the neophytes, it is desirable that they be helped carefully and familiarly in all circumstances by the community of the faithful, by their godparents and by their pastors. Great care should be taken that they obtain full and joyful insertion into the life of the community.

236. At Sunday Masses throughout the Easter season, the neophytes should keep their special places among the faithful. All the neophytes should take part in the Mass with their godparents. They should be mentioned in the homily and in the general intercessions.

237. To close the period of postbaptismal catechesis, at the end of the Easter season, around Pentecost, some form of celebration is held, adding external festivities according to local customs.

238. On the anniversary of their baptism, it is desirable that the neophytes gather together again to give thanks to God, to share their spiritual experience with one another, and to gain new strength.

239. To develop pastoral contact with the new members of his church, the bishop should make sure, especially if he cannot preside at

the sacrament of initiation, that at least once a year he meets the newly baptized and presides at a celebration of the eucharist. At this Mass they may receive communion under both species.

Appendix 2

Excerpts from *Rite of Christian Initiation of Adults: Complete Text of the Rite Together with Additional Rites Approved for Use in the Dioceses of the United States of America (1988)*

Introduction

7.4. The final period extends through the whole Easter season and is devoted to the postbaptismal catechesis or mystagogy. It is a time for deepening the Christian experience, for spiritual growth, and for entering more fully into the life and unity of the community.

8. The whole initiation must bear a markedly paschal character, since the initiation of Christians is the first sacramental sharing in Christ's dying and rising and since, in addition, the period of purification and enlightenment ordinarily coincides with Lent and the period of postbaptismal catechesis or mystagogy with the Easter season.

9.5. During the period immediately after baptism, the faithful should take part in the Masses for neophytes, that is, the Sunday Masses of the Easter season, welcome the neophytes with open arms in charity, and help them to feel more at home in the community of the baptized.

11. Their godparents accompany the candidates ... during the period of mystagogy. ... They continue to be important during the time after reception of the sacraments when the neophytes need to be assisted so that they remain true to their baptismal promises.

25. On all the Sundays of the Easter season after Easter Sunday, the so-called Masses for neophytes are to be scheduled. The entire

community and the newly baptized with their godparents should be encouraged to participate.

Part I: Christian Initiation of Adults

Outline for Christian Initiation of Adults

Period of Postbaptismal Catechesis or Mystagogy: This is the time, usually the Easter season, following the celebration of initiation, during which the newly initiated experience being fully a part of the Christian community by means of pertinent catechesis and particularly by participation with all the faithful in the Sunday eucharistic celebration.

Period of Postbaptismal Catechesis or Mystagogy

> You are a chosen race, a royal priesthood, a holy people; praise God who called you out of darkness and into his marvelous light.

244. The third step of Christian initiation, the celebration of the sacraments, is followed by the final period, the period of postbaptismal catechesis or mystagogy. This is a time for the community and the neophytes together to grow in deepening their grasp of the paschal mystery and in making it part of their lives through meditation on the Gospel, sharing in the eucharist, and doing the works of charity. To strengthen the neophytes as they begin to walk in newness of life, the community of the faithful, their godparents, and their parish priests (pastors) should give them thoughtful and friendly help.

245. The neophytes are, as the term "mystagogy" suggests, introduced into a fuller and more effective understanding of mysteries through the Gospel message they have learned and above all through their experience of the sacraments they have received. For they have truly been renewed in mind, tasted more deeply the sweetness of God's words, received the fellowship of the Holy Spirit, and grown to know the goodness of the Lord. Out of this experience, which belongs to

Christians and increases as it is lived, they derive a new perception of the faith, of the church, and of the world.

246. Just as their new participation in the sacraments enlightens the neophytes' understanding of the Scriptures, so too it increases their contact with the rest of the faithful and has an impact on the experience of the community. As a result, interaction between the neophytes and the faithful is made easier and more beneficial. The period of postbaptismal catechesis is of great significance for both the neophytes and the rest of the faithful. Through it the neophytes, with the help of their godparents, should experience a full and joyful welcome into the community and enter into closer ties with the other faithful. The faithful, in turn, should derive from it a renewal of inspiration and outlook.

247. Since the distinctive spirit and power of the period of postbaptismal catechesis or mystagogy derive from the new, personal experience of the sacraments and of the community, its main setting is the so-called Masses for neophytes, that is, the Sunday Masses of the Easter season. Besides being occasions for the newly baptized to gather with the community and share in the mysteries, these celebrations include particularly suitable readings from the Lectionary, especially the readings for Year A. Even when Christian initiation has been celebrated outside the usual times, the texts for these Sunday Masses of the Easter season may be used.

248. All the neophytes and their godparents should make an effort to take part in the Masses for the neophytes and the entire local community should be invited to participate with them. Special places in the congregation are to be reserved for the neophytes and their godparents. The homily and, as circumstances suggest, the general intercessions should take into account the presence and needs of the neophytes.

249. To close the period of postbaptismal catechesis, some sort of celebration should be held at the end of the Easter season near Pentecost Sunday; festivities in keeping with local custom may accompany the occasion.

250. On the anniversary of their baptism the neophytes should be brought together in order to give thanks to God, to share with one another their spiritual experiences, and to renew their commitment.

251. To show his pastoral concern for these new members of the church, the bishop, particularly if he was unable to preside at the sacraments of initiation himself, should arrange, if possible, to meet the recently baptized at least once in the year and to preside at a celebration of the eucharist with them. At this Mass they may receive holy communion under both kinds.

Part II : Rites for Particular Circumstances

Christian Initiation of Children who have Reached Catechetical Age

330. A period of postbaptismal catechesis or mystagogy should be provided to assist the young neophytes and their companions who have completed their Christian initiation. This period can be arranged by an adaptation of the guidelines given for adults (nos. 244–251).

Christian Initiation of Adults in Exceptional Circumstances

335. When this expanded form of initiation is arranged, care should be taken to ensure that: ...
    3. after receiving the sacraments the neophyte has the benefit of a period of postbaptismal catechesis, if at all possible.

Preparation of Uncatechized Adults for Confirmation and Eucharist

410. These adults will complete their Christian formation and become fully integrated into the community by going through the period of postbaptismal catechesis or mystagogy with the newly baptized members of the Christian community.

National Statutes for the Catechumenate

21. Candidates who have received their formation in an abbreviated catechumenate should receive the sacraments of Christian

initiation at the Easter Vigil, if possible, together with candidates who have participated in the more extended catechumenate. They should also participate in the period of mystagogy, to the extent possible.

22. After the completion of their Christian initiation in the sacraments of baptism, confirmation, and eucharist, the neophytes should begin the period of mystagogy by participating in the principal Sunday eucharist of the community throughout the Easter season, which ends on Pentecost Sunday. They should do this as a body in company with their godparents and those who have assisted in their Christian formation.

23. Under the moderation of the diocesan bishop, the mystagogy should embrace a deepening understanding of the mysteries of baptism, confirmation, and the eucharist, and especially of the eucharist as the continuing celebration of faith and conversion.

24. After the immediate mystagogy or postbaptismal catechesis during the Easter season, the program for the neophytes should extend until the anniversary of Christian initiation, with at least monthly assemblies of the neophytes for their deeper Christian formation and incorporation into the full life of the Christian community.

Code of Canon Law

789. Through a suitable instruction neophytes are to be formed to a more thorough understanding of the Gospel truth and the baptismal duties to be fulfilled; they are to be imbued with a love of Christ and of His church.

Notes

Introduction

1. The number following a church document title refers to the paragraph number.

2. Throughout this introduction, the term *mystagogy* can be understood as synonymous with *postbaptismal catechesis*. This understanding will change as the book progresses.

3. The North American Forum on the Catechumenate is an international network of pastoral ministers, liturgists, catechists, and theologians united to share the vision and practice of the *Rite of Christian Initiation of Adults*. The forum sponsors institutes that help pastoral ministers understand the vision and develop pastoral skills for the implementation of the *Rite of Christian Initiation of Adults*. The Beginnings and Beyond Institutes are designed with separate tracks for the inexperienced (Beginnings) and the experienced (Beyond) pastoral minister. I attended the Beyond sessions at the Institute hosted by the Diocese of Gary during the summer of 1984.

4. *Complete text.* The English translation, original texts, and additional notes by the International Commission on English in the Liturgy, 1985, are from the original Latin *Ordo initiationis christianae adultorum*. Additional rites, texts, and *National Statutes for the Catechumenate* were prepared by the Bishops' Committee on the Liturgy of the National Conference of Catholic Bishops, 1988. Hereafter referred to as "RCIA" in footnotes and references and as "the Rite" within the text. The complete text of the paragraphs concerning mystagogy are found in Appendix 2 of this book.

5. A brief description of this method can be found in the discussion of the method on pages 21–24 and in the chart following page 24.

6. The stories related here are not verbatim. The event happened more than ten years ago and has been reconstructed as best as I can recall. This

experience had a profound impact on me, both as a mystagogue and as a member of the Christian faithful and is thus quite memorable for me.

7. The third scrutiny is celebrated on the Fifth Sunday of Lent. The Gospel for that day is John 11:1–45, the story of the raising of Lazarus. Part of this same reading was used as the Gospel at George's funeral the following day.

8. The paschal candle at the Easter Vigil was new. The paschal candle from the previous year was present at the funeral.

9. Throughout this book, the phrase "the Christian initiation of adults" refers to the process described in the RCIA.

10. Numbers refer to paragraphs in the RCIA. No page numbers will be given since different publishers have different paginations. Italics added.

11. The questions were, "From your experience, which of the RCIA stages or rites seems most difficult to understand?" and "Which rite or stage seems most difficult to do?" In the first case, 162 of the 418 responses were mystagogy. In the second question the number rose to 180.

12. These resources include Boyer; Bruns, *Cenacle Sessions* and *Easter Bread*; Regan; and Baumbach.

13. See Appendix 1 for the paragraphs concerning mystagogia in the *RCIA: Provisional text* ... and Appendix 2 for the paragraphs concerning mystagogy in *RCIA: Complete text* ....

14. The catechumenate, which begins with the rite of acceptance into the order of catechumens, includes weekly dismissals from the Sunday Eucharist, celebrations of the word, minor exorcisms, blessings, and anointings of the catechumens and concludes with the rite of election. The period of purification and enlightenment includes three scrutinies, presentations of the Creed and the Lord's Prayer, and preparation rites on Holy Saturday and culminates with the celebration of the sacraments of initiation at the Easter Vigil.

15. These resources include Curtin et al., whose *RCIA: A Practical Approach to Christian Initiation* was one of the first, but by no means the last, such attempts to design a curriculum that is more faithful to the doctrinal tradition than to the liturgical year and the lectionary, and McBride, *A Catholic Learning Guide for Adult Initiation*, which follows this same educational model, including sessions during mystagogy. Other resources have followed the same pattern of educational session. While doctrine is an important part of the tradition, it is by no means the only part that needs to be handed on during the initiation process.

16. Mazza includes mystagogical homilies by Ambrose of Milan, Theodore of Mopsuestia, John Chrysostom, and Cyril of Jerusalem.

17. Hereafter referred to as "RCIA 1974" in footnotes and references and as "the provisional text" or "1974 edition" in the text. See Appendix 1 for paragraphs concerning mystagogy.

18. RCIA 26 states that the initiation process "is normally arranged so that the sacraments will be celebrated during the Easter Vigil. Because of unusual circumstances and pastoral needs," it can be celebrated at some other time. RCIA 247 states, "Even when Christian initiation has been celebrated outside the usual times, the texts for these Sundays Masses of the Easter season may be used." The immediate mystagogy is, therefore, the seven weeks following the celebration of the sacraments, whenever it takes place.

19. RCIA 75 sets the agenda for the catechumenate: "The catechumens learn ... to bear witness to the faith ... and to practice love of neighbor, even at the cost of self-renunciation. ... Catechumens should also learn how to work actively with others to spread the Gospel and build up the church by the witness of their lives and by professing their faith."

20. The North American Forum on the Catechumenate now calls its institute for those with several years of experience with the Christian initiation of adults "The Initiating Community: An Advanced Institute." The title comes from Dunning, "Church As Initiating Community," 9–10.

21. The vision of the Rite expresses an idealized view. It is not descriptive but proscriptive. It affirms and challenges the present praxis.

22. These are my questions. They arise from my conversation with the texts of the Rite, the texts of other authors, and the text of my own experience. They are based on this interpreter's experience of the conversation.

> [T]he model of conversation, as Gadamer correctly insists, is also in fact applicable to our experience of interpretation of texts. For if interpreters allow the claim of the text to serious attention to provoke their questioning, then they enter into the logic of question and response. And that logic is nothing other than the particular form which the to-and-fro movement of this singular game, the conversation, takes. The kind of interaction which occurs when we converse is, in fact, the interaction whereby the subject matter, not our own subjectivity, is allowed to take over. If we cannot converse, if we cannot allow for the demands of any subject matter—any questions provoked by the claim of attention of the text—then we cannot interpret. But if we have even once entered into any genuine

conversation, then we are willing to admit that conversation can be a model for the process of interpretation itself (Tracy 159).

The conversation is not complete. The experience of neophytes and mystagogues in several parishes will enter the conversation in the following chapter. The questions are only beginning, and the response is yet to come as the conversation continues throughout this book.

23. The aphorism ascribed to Prosper of Aquitaine's Indiculus (435–442), *lex orandi, lex credendi*, has been considered a truism by many liturgical theologians. How we pray reflects how we believe, and how we believe reflects how we pray.

24. See Dunning, *Echoing God's Word*, for a discussion of the difference between teaching doctrine and passing on the faith.

25. These evaluations often included asking the participants to rate individual sessions on a scale of one to five, from "excellent to poor" or from "extremely helpful to not very helpful." There was also room for comments. Generally the workshops were rated between excellent and very good. Comments often included phrases such as "I learned a lot," "Great presentation," "Very insightful." These kinds of comments don't really tell me what was learned or not learned, what methods were helpful or not helpful. They seem to be based on how the participants experienced the workshop, not what they learned from it. While I believe it is important for the participants to have a good experience during a workshop, I also believe that it important that they have learned a new skill or new information that will change their behavior (preferably for the better).

26. Note that in this context, the word *behavior* refers to both thoughts and actions. The ways in which we think about something are considered behaviors when using methods that come from a behavioral psychology background.

27. *Music in Catholic Worship* states, "Faith grows when it is well expressed in celebration. Good celebrations foster and nourish faith. Poor celebrations may weaken and destroy it" (6). Because mystagogy is fundamentally a liturgical experience, the same might be said of mystagogical experiences.

Chapter 1

1. These include staff and team members of the North American Forum on the Catechumenate as well as persons whom I had known for several years and who shared a concern for the implementation of the Rite with me.

2. Interviews took place in five parishes, although only three parishes are being used in this study. The criteria for choosing the three parishes was simply the order in which the parishes were visited. After reviewing all of the interviews, it became apparent that while additional data would be available by including all five parishes, the insights gained from the interviews would substantially remain the same by including only the first three parishes.

3. In order to give some geographical or regional context to the descriptions, the names of the (arch)dioceses are correct. The parish names are fictitious, although the saints (all of them early mystagogues) for whom they are renamed are not.

4. In correspondence with the parish director of Christian initiation, I had specifically asked to meet with recent neophytes or those who had been baptized no more than two years. The director at St. Ambrose of Milan Parish felt that an interview with this particular convert of five years would be helpful. Though beyond the original parameters set for this study, I thought I might learn something from him too. Several recent neophytes were willing but unable to meet with me during the time I visited this parish. I use the word *convert* here in the same sense as it is used in the NSC. A convert is a person who has moved from unbelief to belief, from being unbaptized to being baptized. The word *neophyte* is reserved for persons who have been baptized less than one year, though in this book I will occasionally use it for persons baptized a few months more than a year. In this particular case, this convert is not a neophyte because he was baptized more than five years ago.

5. Descriptions of parishes are based on on-site visits to each parish, a written questionnaire answered by the parish director prior to my visit, and interviews with the director, parish initiation team, and one to six neophytes. Each on-site visit lasted at least three days. Other materials, like parish bulletins, brochures, or booklets about the parish and/or its initiation process also informed the descriptions that follow. I also participated in the Sunday Eucharist as part of each parish visit.

6. This list comes from the parish bulletin as well as from conversations with a number of the people who hold these positions.

7. The school-year model for implementing the RCIA truncates the initiation process to a schedule that mirrors the school year. The period of inquiry begins near the beginning of the school year, and the process ends with mystagogy at the end of the school year. The period of the catechumenate is thus shortened to less than six months rather than the full year or more called for in the NSC (6).

8. The title of the rite has been abbreviated in the text. The full title is "Celebration of the Rite of Acceptance into the Order of Catechumens and the Rite of Welcoming Baptized but Previously Uncatechized Adults Who Are Preparing for Confirmation and/or Eucharist or Reception into the Full Communion of the Catholic Church." This ritual is found in RCIA 505.

9. This means that catechumens are not dismissed during the period of the catechumenate, except at the beginning when the rite of acceptance and welcoming is celebrated. Because rites are celebrated on the First through the Fifth Sundays of Lent, the Elect are dismissed every Sunday during Lent except for Passion/Palm Sunday. Candidates for full communion are always dismissed along with catechumens and the Elect. The Elect are not dismissed from the celebration of the Lord's Supper on Holy Thursday nor from the celebration of the Lord's Passion on Good Friday.

10. Catechumens or candidates for full communion who at that time do not feel they are ready to continue or who for canonical reasons may not complete their initiation at the approaching Easter Vigil may join the process when it begins again the following September.

11. The title of this rite has been abbreviated in the text. The full title is "Parish Celebration for Sending Catechumens for election and Candidates for Recognition by the Bishop [Optional]." This ritual is found in RCIA 530–546.

12. The title of this rite has been abbreviated in the text. The full title is "Celebration of the Rite of election of Catechumens and of the Call to Continuing Conversion of Candidates Who Are Preparing for Confirmation and/or Reception into the Full Communion of the Catholic Church." This ritual is found in RCIA 547–561.

13. Parishioners are invited to form small faith-sharing groups each year during Lent. These groups meet in the homes of parishioners and reflect on the Lenten Scriptures. The Elect and the candidates for full communion, along with their sponsors, each join with one of these groups.

14. This rehearsal includes all the ministers, the catechumens and candidates for full communion, and their sponsors. They walk through the ritual,

rehearsing where they will stand and what physical movements will take place as part of the initiation ritual at the Easter Vigil.

15. The rite of acceptance, the rite of sending, the rite of election, and the scrutinies are followed by a gathering during which the catechumens, the candidates for full communion, and their sponsors reflect on the questions just presented in the previous quotation.

16. Mauck makes the distinction between immersion and submersion fonts in *Shaping a House for the Church*. An *immersion* font is designed for adults to stand or kneel in while water is poured over them by the presider. A *submersion* font is designed so that an adult can be completely plunged beneath the water during baptism.

17. The music of David Haas, Marty Haugen, and Michael Joncas—all from the local area—forms the basis of the parish repertoire.

18. The list of pastoral associates comes from the front page of the parish bulletin, and I was introduced to several of them during my visit to the parish.

19. This is a full-time staff position at St. Cyril of Jerusalem Parish, with about 25 percent of the time dedicated to the implementation of the RCIA.

20. The parish director of the RCIA described these positions as follows: The *person responsible for sponsors* recruits, trains, and assists the sponsors in their ministry. *Faith sharers* tell their own stories of how they have experienced God in their lives or how they live out their faith at a catechetical session, either during the precatechumenate or the catechumenate. They each participate in one and only one catechetical session, and generally, there is one at each session. *Prayer partners* offer to keep a particular candidate in prayer throughout the initiation process, often sending a note to the candidate assuring the person of their prayerful concern. Sponsors, faith sharers, and prayer partners are not considered members of the initiation team but are support staff who assist the candidates in their initiation experience.

21. See note 7 in this chapter.

22. The room is open, with windows bringing in both the light and the natural plant life that is landscaped just outside the windows. It has a contemporary living room area where people can gather for informal conversation. There are several live plants around the room. Tables and comfortable meeting chairs are available for various arrangements that might be needed.

23. See note 8 in this chapter and RCIA 505.

24. Those who are already baptized are signed while standing in the aisles of the church, surrounded by the assembly of those who are already baptized.

The unbaptized are signed in the sanctuary, where they are set apart as those approaching the sacraments of initiation for the first time.

25. See note 13 in this chapter for a brief description of faith sharing.

26. See note 12 in this chapter and RCIA 547.

27. The penitential rite, or scrutiny (RCIA 459–486), is an optional rite provided only in the adaptation of the RCIA for the Dioceses of the United States of America and may be celebrated on the Second Sunday of Lent. The parish initiation team at St. Cyril Parish has chosen not to celebrate this optional rite.

28. This book contains background information about Lent and mystagogy as well as outlines of sessions for the Elect (during Lent) and for neophytes (during the Easter season). Each mystagogy session begins with a prayer, Scripture reading, questions for reflection that relate the Scripture with the neophyte's own life experience, small- and large-group sharing, and a closing prayer experience. The Scripture reading is one of those the neophytes would have already heard at the Sunday Eucharist that week.

29. The pastoral associate for adult formation and RCIA also coordinates a program of small Christian communities in the parish. Neophytes and those who were received into the full communion of the Catholic Church are invited to form their own small community. When I conducted the interviews at St. Cyril's, this new group had recently met for the first time, and most of those invited both participated in the initial gathering and committed themselves to form a small Christian community. Some of these groups from previous years continue to gather for faith sharing.

30. In the year-round model, the period of inquiry begins when someone expresses an interest in entering the initiation process and continues until the person has had an initial experience of conversion. Persons are ministered as individuals rather than groups. Everyone moves through the process at his or her own pace. Thus, some people become catechumens at one time while others remain inquirers for a longer time. The catechumenate is also flexible in duration, beginning with the rite of acceptance, which might be celebrated three or more times a year in a given parish. Catechumens generally spend a year or more in the catechumenate before becoming the Elect. The period of purification and enlightenment and the period of mystagogy continue to correspond to Lent and the first year after the sacraments of initiation are celebrated. In this model, there are generally some people in the precatechumenate and others in the catechumenate throughout the year. This model corresponds more faithfully to the RCIA and the NSC.

31. This is based on comments made by those I interviewed during my visit to St. Cyril of Jerusalem Parish. I did not notice the pattern of these comments, however, until I listened to all of the taped interviews from this parish several months later.

32. The consultant for catechist formation works with catechists in a variety of parish program. She especially assists in the training of catechists for the RCIA and Re-membering Church.

33. These include African Americans and immigrants from Asia and Latin America.

34. Baptism by infusion is the process by which water is poured over the head of the person being baptized. During baptism by immersion, the person is actually in the font, though not necessarily submerged below the water.

35. The priest in residence lives with the pastor and pastor emeritus and assists with sacramental celebrations. He has no other duties in the parish because he works full-time in a diocesan office.

36. Three times each week, the parish provides opportunities for adults to gather to reflect on the Scriptures from the Sunday liturgy.

37. The Little Rock Scripture Study was designed by the office of religious education of the diocese of Little Rock, Arkansas. Individual books of the Bible are studied with a focus both on contemporary biblical studies and on what the Scriptures have to say to Catholic Christians today. Sessions include time for personal reflection, prayer, input (either in person or via videotape by someone who has studied the Scriptures), and discussion. It is now published by The Liturgical Press.

38. The Network of Prayer is a group of parishioners who gather together for prayer and who keep in contact via telephone with each other and with seniors who cannot leave their homes. The telephone network offers security and comfort to those who are often alone and in need of some human contact on a regular basis.

39. New Visions Ministry is a support group for separated and divorced Catholics.

40. Re-membering Church is the name given to a process for reconciling members who have for some reason left the Catholic Church or ceased to practice their faith. The process is inspired by the Order of Penitents from the fourth century and the RCIA today.

41. The St. Vincent de Paul Society offers assistance to persons in need by operating a food pantry and offering other forms of support and encouragement.

42. *The RCIA Journey in Faith*, available from Franciscan Communications, and *Prayer, Beliefs, and Precepts of the Catholic Church*, compiled by a previous director of adult initiation at St. John Chrysostom Parish.

43. Or for those who are already baptized, to celebrate the rite of welcoming the candidates.

44. Prayer sponsors are members of the parish who make a commitment to keep a particular catechumen or candidate in prayer throughout the process. They often send notes of encouragement and meet the person they are sponsoring during the process. Each classroom of the parish school also becomes a prayer sponsor for one or more of the catechumens and candidates, praying for and sending words of support to the one whom they are sponsoring.

45. Members of the initiation team look for indications of conversion described in RCIA 75.2 (that is, they "turn more readily to God in prayer, ... bear witness to the faith, in all things, ... keep their hopes set on Christ, ... follow supernatural inspiration in their deeds, and ... practice love of neighbor, even at the cost of self-renunciation." Generally, only those who have been catechumens for a minimum of six months are invited to this discernment, though in individual cases, the time may be shorter or longer. Most have been catechumens or candidates for close to a full year by the time they celebrate the sacraments of initiation.

46. Only the elect preparing for baptism at the upcoming Easter Vigil are scrutinized.

47. One candidate was received into the full communion of the Catholic Church earlier in the year. After some discernment involving the candidate and members of the initiation team, including the pastor, it was decided that for this person the reception of baptized Christians into the full communion of the Catholic Church (RCIA 473–504) was more suitable than the preparation of uncatechized adults for confirmation and Eucharist (RCIA 400–472). Because the members of the initiation team are now more aware of the distinctions presented by the Rite between those who are catechized and those who are uncatechized, this situation is likely to arise again.

Chapter 2

1. My interviews with neophytes and mystagogues at two other parishes, both located in the Diocese of Orlando and not described in the previous chapter, have also influenced the development and articulation of the

following insights. Their experiences were so similar to those already described at St. Ambrose, St. Cyril, and St. John Chrysostom parishes that it would have been redundant to include them in the previous chapter. While adding little new data to this project, these additional interviews confirmed and nuanced some of what I am about to describe. These two parishes, like St. John Chrysostom Parish, follow a year-round model of initiation.

2. The Echoing God's Word Institute is sponsored by the North American Forum on the Catechumenate. It was originally designed under the leadership of James B. Dunning, who authored a book with the same title.

3. Lectionary-based catechesis begins with the Scripture readings of the lectionary, which set the theme for the catechetical session. "The mission of catechesis, therefore, is to introduce people to God and not just to texts and doctrines about God" (Dunning, *Echoing God's Word*, 54). The mission of lectionary-based catechesis is to introduce people to God through reflection on the word of God proclaimed at liturgy. Other catechetical methods often focus on the handing on of the doctrines of the church, which can at times be experienced more like teaching people about God rather than helping them to develop a relationship with God.

Chapter 3

1. While the preaching of Zeno of Verona (d. 370) and Augustine of Hippo (d. 430) are also historically significant, I have chosen to limit the focus of this book to those who preached during the final quarter of the fourth century. Like several other authors (e.g., Riley, Mazza, and Yarnold), I have limited this investigation to these four ancient mystagogues:

> In the fourth century, there emerged four church fathers whose
> baptismal homilies were inspiring mystagogical presentations that
> enabled the neophytes to relate their own experience of the
> sacraments to the mysteries of initiation into the church. These
> were Cyril of Jerusalem, Ambrose of Milan, John Chrysostom and
> Theodore of Mopsuestia. The work of these fathers can be described
> as the work of mystagogy (Baumbach 7).

2. Hippolytus was a priest in Rome, elected bishop of Rome by one faction, while Pontian was elected by another (around 231). As such, he is often

referred to as an antipope. Before his death, both he and Pontian were exiled from Rome, and they reconciled and resigned their positions so that a single bishop might be elected to serve the church. Both were martyred in 235 and venerated as saints by the beginning of the fourth century. Eucharistic Prayer II of the Roman Missal of Paul VI is based in large measure on the eucharistic prayer found in the *Apostolic Tradition*, which is generally credited to Hippolytus.

3. *Hippolytus: A Text for Students* is hereafter referred to as AT followed by the paragraph numbers found in the edition listed in the bibliography.

4. Paul Bradshaw (3–17) and others have raised serious questions about the original authorship and the dating of the *Apostolic Tradition*. While these recent insights may raise serious questions as to the original authorship, and as to whether the *Apostolic Tradition* can be said to have had a single author, there is little doubt that the extant text could be dated any later than the *Apostolic Constitutions*, "usually regarded as having been compiled c. 375–380" (Bradshaw 5). From internal evidence and comparisons with other ancient texts, the section on initiation "would have had to have been completed before the end of the first quarter of the fourth century" (14). Though I treat the *Apostolic Tradition* as if composed by Hippolytus, I am aware that multiple authors and redactors were probably involved. However, the new dating of the *Apostolic Tradition* continues to permit one to see the *Apostolic Tradition* as a source for or inspiration behind the practices of the late-fourth-century mystagogues treated later in this book.

5. Both Mazza (150) and Yarnold (69) put Cyril's death in 387, whereas Quasten (362) and Wilkinson (9) put it in the previous year.

6. A reconstruction of the text of the Jerusalem Creed can be found in McCauley and Stephenson, vol. 1, 63–64.

7. Yarnold believes the *Catecheses* were preached in 348 (69), whereas Stephenson places them in the following year (McCauley and Stephenson, vol. 1, 1). Cross (*Oxford Dictionary* 369) revised his earlier claim of 347 in favor of 350.

8. Yarnold (69) is convinced the MC were preached by Cyril, citing an unpublished thesis submitted to Oxford University titled *The Authorship of the Mystagogic Catecheses attributed to St. Cyril of Jerusalem* (1992). Mazza, on the other hand, is equally convinced that they were preached by Cyril's immediate successor as bishop of Jerusalem, John (150). Cross agrees with Yarnold, claiming that the assertion that John preached the MC is "perhaps [made] on insufficient grounds" (*St. Cyril of Jerusalem's Lectures* 369). Since these and

other scholars continue to disagree as to the authorship of the MC, it is impossible to date them with any certainty, except to say that if they were preached by Cyril, it was before he died in 387, and if by John, sometime after he became bishop that same year.

9. The extant texts are, however, from very different years because the *Catecheses* were preached when Cyril was still a presbyter (that is, before 350) and the *Mystagogic Catecheses* were preached after he had become a bishop. See notes 10 and 11.

10. This translation of the *Mystagogic Catecheses* is based on that prepared by P. G. Walsh in Cross's *St. Cyril of Jerusalem's Lectures on the Christian Sacraments*, with minor changes by Yarnold in *The Awe-Inspiring Rites of Initiation*, 70–97. Excerpts from the MC are followed by the sermon and paragraph numbers from Yarnold's edition.

11. From 1 Peter, Romans, 1 John, and 1 Corinthians.

12. Cross (*Oxford Dictionary*) calls her *Etheria*, though the arguments in favor of *Egeria* seem rather convincing. See especially Wilkinson (235–236) and Gingras (2–7).

13. Wilkinson (237–239) believes she visited Palestine from 381 to 384, while Gingras (12–15) dates the trip at least ten years later, and Cross (473) dates it simply as "at the end of the 4th century."

14. This same ritual pattern is repeated over and over again as Egeria describes the various rites she witnessed in Jerusalem.

15. The cross is located at the corner of a courtyard between the church built by Constantine over the place where the crucifixion is believed to have taken place (the Martyrium) and the Anastasis (a building around the tomb where the body of Jesus is thought to have been entombed).

16. Egeria uses the word *infantes*. Gingras translates this as *neophytes*. Wilkinson uses the word "*infants*" (always in quotation marks), "a word which means rather that they were newborn babes in Christ than that they were infants by age" (34).

17. Yarnold puts the date at 391 (98). Mazza claims they were "probably written about 380–390" (14). Deferrari simply states that they were "probably written earlier" than 387 (xix).

18. Numerous scholars (e.g., Deferrari, Mazza, and Yarnold) agree that the text of *On the Sacraments* are the notes taken down and compiled by those who heard Ambrose's preaching during Easter week, whereas the text of *On the Mysteries* was probably written by Ambrose for publication after he had preached the sermons *On the Sacraments*.

19. Cyril of Jerusalem begins his mystagogy with the following:

> For some time now, true and beloved children of the church, I have
> desired to discourse to you on these spiritual and celestial
> mysteries. But I well knew that visual testimony is more
> trustworthy than mere hearsay, and therefore I awaited this chance
> of finding you more amenable to my words, so that out of your
> personal experience I could lead you into the brighter and more
> fragrant meadow of Paradise on earth. The moment is especially
> auspicious, since you became receptive to the more heavenly
> mysteries when you were accounted worth of divine and vitalizing
> baptism. It remains therefore to lay before you a feast of more
> perfect instruction; so let me give you careful schooling in this so
> that you may know the true significance of what happened to you
> on the evening of your baptism (MC 1, 1).

20. All quotations from *On the Sacraments* will be from James Walsh's translation as found in Yarnold. They are noted as "OS" followed by the sermon number and the paragraph number(s).

21. For a description of what has been called the *disciplina arcane*, see Yarnold 55–59.

22. Here Ambrose also explains why the nostrils are touched rather than the mouth (as in the Scripture passage on which this ritual is based).

23. G. Francesconi, *Storia e simbolo* (Brescia, 1981) 329, as cited in Mazza 34.

24. All citations of *Baptismal Instructions* will be noted as "BI" followed by the instruction number and the paragraph number(s). All quotations are from Harkins; this same translation is cited in Yarnold and Mazza.

25. Mazza claims they were probably preached at Tarsus or Mopsuestia while Theodore was still a presbyter (45). Yarnold, however, claims that "it is probably during his time at Antioch that he preached the 16 catechetical sermons" (165).

26. Theodore was accused of being a Nestorian because when referring to the incarnation he often used the phrase "assuming a man" rather than the scriptural and more orthodox phrase "becoming flesh."

27. Some scholars divide the homilies based on the topics, thus considering the homily on the Lord's Prayer to be part of the prebaptismal instruction. See Yarnold 165.

28. Mazza (45) notes that the Syriac manuscript contains the following addition by the Syrian translator at end of Theodore's tenth catechetical homily:

> End of the writing down of the ten homilies on the explanation of the creed by His Excellency Mar Theodore, friend of Christ, bishop, and interpreter of the divine things.

This same manuscript also contains the following prayer, added by the translator, at the beginning of Theodore's eleventh catechetical homily:

> By your power, our Lord Jesus Christ, we begin to write down the explanation of the mysteries by the same Mar Theodore. Lord, help me and enable me to reach the end.

29. The *Baptismal Homilies* of Theodore of Mopsuestia will be cited from Mingana's translations and include the volume and page numbers (his text has no paragraph numbers). While Yarnold's translation (168–250) is more recent, it is also far from complete and is an English translation of a French translation of the Syriac text originally prepared by Mingana. Excerpts found in Mazza (46–100) are likewise incomplete translations and inadequate for use in this book.

30. During most of those fifteen hundred years, especially the last thousand years, no formal catechumenate or mystagogy for Christian initiation existed.

31. The CSL was actually approved on November 22, 1963, though it was not formally published until almost two weeks later, December 4, 1963. All quotations from this document are from the translation found in O'Brien, *Documents on the Liturgy, 1968–1979*.

32. The *Decree on the Church's Missionary Activity* was published December 7, 1965, at the end of final session of Vatican II. All Vatican II documents quoted here, except the CSL, are taken from the translation found in Flannery, *Vatican Council II: Constitutions, Decrees, Declarations*.

33. Appendix 1 contains all parts of the RCIA 1974 edition that refer to mystagogy.

34. The *Ordo Initiationis Christianae Adultorum* was issued by the Congregation for Divine Worship on January 6, 1972.

35. ICEL used these terms when the English translation of *Ordo Initiationis Christianae Adultorum* was first issued in 1974. This was an unfortunate use of terms, since many people believed that the rite itself was "initial and

provisional" rather than that the translation was "initial and provisional." Because of the "provisional" nature of the document, many in the Roman Catholic Church, especially among the clergy, continued to follow pastoral practices for adult initiation that were intended to be replaced by those specified in this document.

36. *Christian Initiation: General Introduction,* while not part of the Rite itself, offers a foundation for the Rite that follows.

37. For a summary of the historical record and how it influenced the development of the RCIA, see Catholic Church, National Conference of Catholic Bishops, *Christian Initiation of Adults: A Commentary,* "Historical Perspectives on Initiation," 5–20.

38. Though the catechumenate itself, for all practical purposes, had essentially vanished from common practice in the Roman rite, the Mass of the catechumens remained as the first part of the Eucharist. The naming and signing of the candidate for baptism and the prebaptismal anointing with the oil of catechumens, which at one time were separate parts of the catechumenal process, had become part of a single baptismal ritual.

39. Loosely translated: "The way the church prays is what the church believes."

40. Whether it was the *Baltimore Catechism* for children and adults or *Father Smith Instructs Jackson* for adult converts, the memorization of doctrinal statements was the primary method of passing on the faith for millions of Catholics in the United States just prior to Vatican II. This method assumed that if one knew the doctrine, one would necessarily believe. This could be described as *lex docendi* or *lex cognoscendi, lex credendi* (that is, "what the church teaches or what the church knows, the church believes"). At that time, "faith" was often defined as "intellectual assent to divinely revealed truths." This is a highly cognitive approach that assumes that knowledge of doctrine is synonymous with faith.

41. Even the word *catechesis* is a rediscovery of a language that is based less on Western educational models than on a more holistic approach to learning, especially learning from one's own experience. For a full discussion concerning the distinction between education and catechesis see Dunning, *Echoing God's Word,* Chapter 2.

42. RCIA 1974 (19) gives the clearest description of this formation process, as well as its goals:

1) A fitting formation by priests, deacons, or catechists and other lay persons, given in stages and presented integrally, accommodated to the liturgical year and enriched by celebrations of the word, leads the catechumens to a suitable knowledge of dogmas and precepts and also to an intimate understanding of the mystery of salvation in which they desire to share.

2) Familiar with living the Christian way of life and helped by the example and support of sponsors and godparents and the whole community of the faithful, the catechumens will learn to pray to God more easily, to witness to the faith, to be constant in the expectation of Christ in all things, to follow supernatural inspirations in their deeds, and to exercise charity toward neighbors to the point of self-renunciation ...

3) By suitable liturgical rites, Mother church helps the catechumens on their journey, cleanses them little by little, and strengthens them with God's blessing ...

4) Since the church's life is apostolic, catechumens should also learn how to work actively with others to spread the Gospel and build up the church by the testimony of their lives and the profession of their faith.

43. See Flannery, *Vatican Council II: Constitutions, Decrees, Declarations*.
44. The rite of becoming catechumens (RCIA 1974 [68–97]) has been renamed in the 1984 edition as the Rite of Acceptance into the Order of Catechumens (48–74).
45. This is explicitly recommended by RCIA 1974 when it says:

Ordinarily, however, when [catechumens] are present in the assembly of the faithful, they should be dismissed in a friendly manner before the eucharistic celebration begins ... they must await their baptism which will bring them into the priestly people and allow them to participate in the Christian worship of the new covenant (19.3).

46. "Simple Rite of Adult Initiation," RCIA 1974 (240–277). Paragraph 240 states:

> In extraordinary circumstances, when the candidate cannot go through all the stages of initiation, or when the local ordinary, judging that the candidate is sincere in his [sic] conversion to Christianity and in his religious maturity, permits him to receive baptism without delay, the bishop may allow this simple rite to be used in individual cases.

47. All ritual texts used in the liturgy of the Roman Catholic Church begin with an original text approved by the Sacred Congregation for Worship and Sacraments. This document is called the *editio typico* and is usually written in Latin. All translations are based on this original text, though bishops' conferences are free to submit additional texts to supplement those found in the *editio typico*.

48. The initiation process for these people includes only eleven paragraphs in RCIA 1974, whereas whole new rituals, listed above, are included with the adaptations for the church in the United States.

49. The Greek word *leitourgía* comes from two other Greek words meaning "the work of the people."

50. The NSC was approved by the National Conference of Catholic Bishops on November 11, 1986. See RCIA Appendix III for all the statutes and Appendix 2 of this book for those that specifically pertain to mystagogy.

51. In *Music in Catholic Worship* (6), the U.S. bishops claim, "Faith grows when it is well expressed in celebration. Good celebrations foster and nourish faith. Poor celebrations may weaken or destroy it."

52. When catechumens are dismissed from the liturgy, they first reflect on what they heard in the Liturgy of the Word. When the Elect are dismissed, they first reflect on the experience of becoming the Elect or of being scrutinized. When neophytes gather, they first reflect on their experience of becoming Christian through their experience of baptism, confirmation, and Eucharist.

53. RCIA 75.2 states that catechumens are to "become more familiar with the Christian way of life, ... to bear witness to the faith, ... and to practice love of neighbor, even at the cost of self-renunciation." RCIA 244 calls "the community and the neophytes together to grow in deepening their grasp of the paschal mystery ... [by] doing works of charity."

54. This is especially true as ministers consider which rites are appropriate for the particular circumstances of the particular candidates. Whether a candidate is baptized or unbaptized, catechized or uncatechized are important considerations.

Chapter 4

1. Tracy (note 50, pages 21–22) describes the conversational method used throughout this book.
2. Though the testimony of only fifteen of the recent neophytes is a part of the written examination of the present practices (described in Chapter 1), ten other neophytes were interviewed as part of the research for this project. Their testimony reinforced but did not substantially alter the conclusions drawn from the testimony of the first fifteen neophytes interviewed.
3. Robert Schreiter writes in *The New Catholicity*:

> "Flow" is a term that has come to be used in sociology, anthropology, and communications science to denote cultural and ritual movements, a circulation of information that is patently visible yet hard to define. Flows move across geographic and other cultural boundaries, and, like a river, define a route, change the landscape, and leave behind sediment and silt that enrich the local ecology. ...
> Theological flows, then, are theological discourses that, while not uniform or systemic, represent a series of linked mutually intelligible discourses. ... They are theological discourses, that is, they speak out of the realm of religious beliefs and practices. They are not uniform or systemic, because of their commitment to specific cultural and social settings. Yet they are intelligible to discourses in other cultural and social settings (15).

4. Though they used different words to describe their experiences of the presence of Christ in these various situations, their experiences pointed to the realities mentioned in the CSL:

> Christ is always present in his church, especially in its liturgical celebrations. He is present in the sacrifice of the Mass, not only in

the person of his minister, ... but especially under the eucharistic elements. By his power he is present in the sacraments, ... He is present in his word, since it is he himself who speaks when the holy Scriptures are read in the church. He is present, lastly, when the church prays and sings (7).

5. These include Zeno of Verona and Augustine of Hippo, whose writings were examined during my research but are not found in this book.

6. The term *confirmation* would not have been familiar to the fourth-century mystagogues. I use it to refer to the postbaptismal anointing with holy oil or chrism, which today we would call *confirmation*. This anointing was clearly one of the mysteries—what the church would later come to call *sacraments*—with which the mystagogues were concerned.

7. Among the professions that were considered immoral by Hippolytus are the following: "brothel keeper," maker of idols, actor, or anyone who participated in the public games, such as a charioteer, a gladiator, a fighter, or a "public official employed on gladiatorial business," a priest, a soldier, "he who has the power of the sword, or is a magistrate," "a prostitute, a profligate, a eunuch or anyone else who does things of which it is a shame to speak," and numerous others.

8. From the sacramentary, Ash Wednesday, Distribution of Ashes. This might imply something about the connection between the period of purification and enlightenment and the period of postbaptismal catechesis or mystagogy (between Lent and the Easter season). More will be said about this later.

9. "Inquirers often come with a strong desire to share the Eucharist, to be nourished in community by word and sacrament" (see conclusion 3, page 70).

10. RCIA states the following:

The minor exorcisms take place within a celebration of the word of God (92).

The blessings are usually given at the end of a celebration of the word (96).

The anointing ordinarily takes place after the homily in a celebration of the word of God (100).

11. Egeria indicates that the community in Jerusalem celebrated the Eucharist each day of Easter week, but the mystagogy for the neophytes took place at a separate ritual.

12. During the fourth century, it was common practice that only the fully initiated participated in or even discussed the meaning of the eucharistic celebration. This discipline—the *disciplina arcane*—had the effect of increasing both the importance and mystery surrounding the Eucharist. Since one could neither experience nor discuss its meaning until one was initiated, the mystery behind the Eucharist was maximized.

13. For a thorough description of the *disciplina arcane*, see Yarnold 55–59.

14. Since Yarnold chose not to include MC 5, 12–18 in his text, this passage is taken from the translation found in McCauley, Vol. 2.

15. See Dunning, *Echoing God's Word*, especially Chapter 3, for a discussion of the lectionary-based catechesis.

16. Here I do not simply mean the period of postbaptismal catechesis or mystagogy but the entire initiation process, which can be effectively mystagogical.

17. For example, while describing the rite of baptism in great detail, Theodore of Mopsuestia states,

> Immediately after your godfather, who is standing behind you,
> spreads an orarium of linen on the crown of your head, raises you
> and makes you stand erect (BH 6, 47).

18. The Rite also distinguishes between the role of sponsor and the role of godparent. While there are many similarities, and in many cases one and the same person fulfills both these roles, they are distinct in the Rite. Sponsors accompany a candidate from inquiry through the catechumenate. Godparents accompany the candidate from the rite of election through mystagogy and beyond.

19. Here I would include Zeno of Verona and Augustine of Hippo, who also preached both catechetical and mystagogical sermons.

20. The catechetical sermons of Cyril of Jerusalem and John Chrysostom were preached while they were still presbyters. Ambrose of Milan and Theodore of Mopsuestia were already bishops when they preached their catechetical sermons.

21. The immediate mystagogy of the Easter season and the first full year after initiation today as opposed to one week of special celebrations with preaching by the bishop during the fourth century.

22. See also the *Catecheses* of Cyril of Jerusalem in McCauley Vols. 1 & 2; *Instructions to Catechumens* of John Chrysostom in Schaff; and Mingana Vol. 5.

23. The NSC states,

> After the immediate mystagogy or postbaptismal catechesis during the Easter season, the program for the neophytes should extend until the anniversary of Christian initiation, with at least monthly assemblies of the neophytes for their deeper Christian formation and incorporation into the full life of the Christian community (24).

Chapter 5

1. Note that the CCC speaks of "liturgical catechesis" and then parenthetically states, "It is 'mystagogy.'" I have, therefore, taken the liberty to exchange these terms in this place. I make no claim that the authors of the CCC would approve this revision of their statement.

2. See pages 59–60 about the inquirer's desire to belong and pages 116–118 concerning these new relationships.

3. This is especially evident in the contemporary rite of election, in which the catechumens often experience being part of the larger church, beyond the parish. It is there that they often encounter the diocesan church for the first time and become aware that they are part of a larger phenomenon than simply initiation into a local parish congregation. This experience was described to me by several of the neophytes interviewed for this book.

4. The word *begins* is not to be understood in a chronological sense. Even when mystagogical reflection takes place prior to the celebration of a rite, when the mystagogue helps prepare candidates for a celebration, the focus is on the experience about to take place. It is influenced by the experience of others who have already celebrated the Rite and whose experience forms part of the Christian tradition regarding the meaning of the Rite.

5. *Experience* should be understood in the broadest sense of the word. Mystagogy might begin with the experience of God in nature, the experience of hearing or reading the word of God, the experience of God in oneself or in

another or in the community gathered together, or the experience of a particular ritual. Any experience of God can be the initial catalyst for mystagogy.

6. I owe a debt of gratitude to James B. Dunning, who first asked me these questions as I reflected on my own experience of conversion. I heard these questions again in the preaching of the fourth-century mystagogues, who, while not directly asking the questions, provided not-so-subtle answers to them.

7. Sinwell (29) provides proposed outlines for precatechumenal sessions that include the following:

Topic identified will be from human experience.

Exploring Experience. This section will try to identify experiences of the inquirers relevant to the topic. Participants will be encouraged to reflect and dialogue about these experiences.

Exploring the Word of God. This section will proclaim parts of the word of God that are pertinent to the topic and elicit a response in discussion or reflection. Leaders need to choose the readings or activities appropriate to the group.

Praying. This section will engage the inquirers in different prayer forms in Roman Catholic tradition related to the topic.

Gospel Challenge. This section will present ways of living the message of God's word, thus encouraging conversion. This effort will require reflection in and after session.

8. Donald Neumann made this proposal at The Initiating Community: An Advanced Institute, a workshop sponsored by the North American Forum on the Catechumenate, February 5–8, 1996, Orlando. I have not seen anything in writing concerning this suggestion.

9. See CCC, especially 2443–2449, on love for the poor.

10. The catechumens might also be asked to do ritual or liturgical catechesis on the minor exorcisms, blessings, and anointings.

11. See RCIA 75.1, 75.3, 79, 81–89. The minor exorcisms, blessings, anointings, and presentations all take place within the context of a celebration of the word.

12. CSL states:

> For in the liturgy God is speaking to [God's] people and Christ is
> still proclaiming his Gospel (33).

The GIRM concurs:

> In the readings, explained by the homily, God is speaking to his
> people, opening up to them the mystery of redemption and
> salvation, and nourishing their spirit; Christ is present to the
> faithful through his own word (33).

13. The word *you* is to be understood in both its singular and plural forms.
The question is both personal and communal. Phrasing the question in the
first person, it would become two questions: "What is God's message for
me?" and "What is God's message for us?"

14. The Rite clearly calls for apostolic activity on the part of catechumens
when it states:

> As they become familiar with the Christian way of life and are
> helped by the example and support of sponsors, godparents, and
> the entire Christian community, the catechumens learn to ...
> practice love of neighbor, even at the cost of self-renunciation
> (75.2).

> Since the church's life is apostolic, catechumens should also learn
> how to work actively with others to spread the Gospel and build up
> the church by the witness of their lives and by professing their faith
> (75.4).

The early church, too, had a concern that catechumens be involved in apostolic activity related to the poor when they are asked about their concern for
the widows and others in need. See especially AT 20.

15. Catechumens who are already engaged in one of the helping professions
(e.g., nursing or social work) or are involved in volunteer work among the
needy might be encouraged to reflect on how they are already doing God's
work and how God is revealed to them through their profession or
volunteering.

16. See the section "A Mystagogical Precatechumenate" in this chapter, especially page 146 for further suggestions concerning mystagogical reflection on apostolic activity.

17. Rehearsals for rituals may be necessary, but they should be limited to the participation of sponsors, godparents, and ministers. Candidates, catechumens, and the Elect should experience the rites without rehearsal but confident that those who walk with them and the ministers of the rites know what they are doing. The power of the rite is often diminished if the candidates either know exactly what to expect or are afraid that they might do something wrong during the ritual. Ministers and sponsors who are well prepared will help to alleviate this fear.

18. For example, in preparing for the first scrutiny, Hinman Powell and Sinwell (43) instruct the catechists to include the following during the last twenty minutes of the catechetical session held during the second week of Lent:

1) Briefly explain what "scrutiny" is and what it is not. It is "taking a deep hard look." It is not "pointing fingers!"

2) Invite the elect and godparents to pause and reflect quietly for a moment on where they experience thirst—longing for God, in themselves, in the church, in the world.

3) Invite the elect and godparents to briefly identify (through a brainstorming process) the following:
   places in the world or situations in the world where they see, hear, or experience a thirst for God ...
   situations in the church (local and/or universal) which thirst for God ...
   places in their own hearts, their families, their homes where they long for God ...

The results of the brainstorming are then used to adapt the intercessions that are part of the celebration of the scrutiny to the local community. The Elect are then invited to read the Gospel for the following Sunday as part of their continuing preparation for the celebration of the scrutiny.

19. Chilson suggests prayer experiences that would also help prepare the Elect for the various rituals of the period of purification and enlightenment.

20. In the GNLYC, we are reminded of the following:

> Lent is a preparation for the celebration of Easter. For the Lenten
> liturgy disposes both the catechumens and the faithful to celebrate
> the paschal mystery: catechumens, through the several stages of
> Christian initiation; the faithful, through reminders of their own
> baptism and through penitential practices (27).

The Rite confirms this baptismal focus:

> In the liturgy and liturgical catechesis of Lent the reminder of
> baptism already received or the preparation for its reception, as
> well as the theme of repentance, renew the entire community (138).

21. Bruns, *Cenacle Sessions*; Ellebracht; Hinman Powell and Sinwell; and
other resources offer specific instructions on how to reflect on the various
parts of the Easter Vigil experience.

22. Baumbach; Ramshaw, *Words Around the Fire, Words Around the Table*,
and *Words Around the Font*. One should, however, avoid using these resources simply as workbooks or for private reflection. Mystagogy is always a
communal event and should never be limited to private reading.

23. They likewise assist the entire assembly in reflecting on the experience of
renewal of their baptismal promises and of the Eucharist that they share each
week, the meaning of these experiences, and their responses to these experiences of God at work in their lives.

24. The Rite describes the period of postbaptismal catechesis as follows:

> This is a time for the community and the neophytes together to
> grow in deepening their grasp of the paschal mystery and in
> making it part of their lives through meditation on the Gospel,
> sharing in the eucharist, and *doing the works of charity* (244,
> italics added).

25. See the sections "A Mystagogical Precatechumenate" page 146 and "A
Mystagogical Catechumenate" page 152 for descriptions of mystagogical
reflection on apostolic activity.

26. This would follow a historical pattern, which first developed around what
later became the order of deacons. The deacons' first ministry was one of

service to the poor; only later did a liturgical role develop. The liturgical role developed out of the apostolic—the deacon who worked among the needy was the obvious person to offer prayers for the needy within the liturgical assembly.

27. The Rite states:

> In light of what is said in *Christian Initiation, General Introduction* (no. 7), the people of God, as represented by the local church, should understand and show by their concern that the initiation of adults is the responsibility of all the baptized. Therefore the community must always be fully prepared in the pursuit of its apostolic vocation to give help to those who are searching for Christ. In the various circumstances of daily life, even as in the apostolate, all the followers of Christ have the obligation of spreading the faith according to their abilities. Hence the entire community must help the candidates and the catechumens throughout the process of initiation: during the period of the precatechumenate, the period of the catechumenate, the period of purification and enlightenment, and the period of postbaptismal catechesis or mystagogy (6).

28. Remember the response of Egeria to the Jerusalem community she visited and the response of many of the neophytes to the communities they visited before becoming Christians. All were inspired by the presence of Christ in the midst of the communities they first approached as visitors.

29. I have encountered numerous people who see the Christian initiation of adults as a catechetical process punctuated by rituals. The Rite makes it clear that it is a ritual process that includes catechesis. The interviews with recent neophytes demonstrate that the rituals are both more memorable and significant to the conversion process. The preaching of fourth-century mystagogues also points toward an understanding of Christian initiation as a ritual process with a strong catechetical dimension.

30. In addition to the process described in the U.S. bishops' *Fulfilled in Your Hearing*, Bailey also offers an approach for scriptural interpretation that might assist the preacher in planning a mystagogical homily. He calls it the "theological approach to the hermeneutics for preaching" (193–211).

31. While courses on the theology of initiation are often part of the education of priests, these courses generally do not provide future presiders and

preachers with much personal experience of the rites or of the conversion experience.

32. I would encourage those who preside and preach at the rites of initiation to become as familiar with the rituals as possible and to take time to listen to the stories of conversion that the neophytes in your parishes tell. I would encourage directors of adult initiation to provide opportunities for presiders and preachers to hear one another's stories and be converted by them. I firmly believe that when people hear the witness of what God is doing through the initiation process, they will be converted themselves.

33. Different catechists might take responsibility for different roles throughout the process. All catechists need not perform all the ministries described in this section.

Bibliography

Original Sources

Catholic Church. *Catechism of the Catholic Church*. Chicago: Loyola University Press, 1994.

———. *Code of Canon Law: Latin-English Edition*. Washington, D.C.: Canon Law Society of America, 1983.

———. *Rite of Christian Initiation of Adults: Complete Text of the Rite Together with Additional Rites Approved for Use in the Dioceses of the United States of America*. Prepared by the International Commission on English in the Liturgy and Bishops' Committee on the Liturgy of the National Conference of Catholic Bishops. Washington, D.C.: United States Catholic Conference, 1988.

———. *Rite of Christian Initiation of Adults: Provisional Text Approved for Interim Use in the Dioceses of the United States of America by the Bishops' Committee on the Liturgy and the Executive Committee of the National Conference of Catholic Bishops and confirmed by the Apostolic See*. English Translation by the International Commission on English in the Liturgy. Washington, D.C.: United States Catholic Conference, 1974.

Cody, Aelred. "The Didache: An English Translation." In *The Didache in Context: Essays on Its Text, History and Transmission*. Edited by Clayton N. Jefford. Leiden, The Netherlands: E. J. Brill, 1995. 3–14.

Cross, F. L., ed. and trans. *St. Cyril of Jerusalem's Lectures on the Christian Sacraments*. London: S.P.C.K., 1996.

Cuming, Geoffrey J. *Hippolytus: A Text for Students*. Nottingham: Grove Books, 1976.

Deferrari, Roy Joseph, ed. and trans. *Saint Ambrose: Theological and Dogmatic Works*. The Fathers of the Church, vol. 44. Washington, D.C.: The Catholic University of America Press, 1963.

Easton, Burton Scott, ed. and trans. *The Apostolic Tradition of Hippolytus*. Hamden, Conn.: Archon Books, 1962.

Flannery, Austin, ed. *Vatican Council II: The Conciliar and Post Conciliar Documents*. Collegeville, Minn.: The Liturgical Press, 1975.

––––––. *Vatican Council II: Constitutions, Decrees, Declarations*. Northport, N.Y.: Costello Publishing Co., 1996.

––––––. *Vatican Council II: More Post Conciliar Documents*. Northport, N.Y.: Costello Publishing Co., 1982.

Gifford, Edward Hamilton. *Cyril of Jerusalem, Gregory Nazianzen. Nicene and Post-Nicene Fathers*. Second series. Vol. 7. Edited by Philip Schaff and Henry Wace. Peabody, Mass.: Hendrickson Pub., Inc., 1995. Originally published by Christian Literature Pub. Co., 1889.

Gingras, George E., ed. and trans. *Egeria: Diary of a Pilgrimage*. Ancient Christian Writers: Works of the Fathers in Translation, no. 38. Edited by Johannes Quasten, Walter J. Burghardt, and Thomas Comerford Lawler. New York: Newman Press, 1970.

Harkins, Paul W., ed. and trans. *St. John Chrysostom: Baptismal Instructions*. Ancient Christian Writers: Works of the Fathers in Translation, no. 31. Edited by Johannes Quasten and Walter J. Burghardt. Westminster, Md.: The Newman Press, 1963.

Hoffman, Elizabeth, ed. *The Liturgy Documents*. Chicago: Liturgy Training Publications, 1991.

Jeanes, Gordon P. *The Day Has Come! Easter and Baptism in Zeno of Verona*. Collegeville, Minn.: The Liturgical Press, 1995.

McCauley, Leo P., and Anthony A. Stephenson, eds. and trans. *The Works of Saint Cyril of Jerusalem, Vol. 1*. The Fathers of the Church, vol. 61. Washington, D.C.: The Catholic University of America Press, 1969.

––––––. *The Works of Saint Cyril of Jerusalem, Vol. 2*. The Fathers of the Church, vol. 64. Edited by Bernard M. Peebles et al. Washington, D.C.: The Catholic University of America Press, 1970.

Mingana, Alphonse, ed. and trans. *Commentary of Theodore of Mopsuestia on the Lord's Prayer and on the Sacraments of Bap-*

tism and Eucharist. Woodbrooke Studies: Christian Documents Edited and Translated with a Critical Apparatus, vol. 6. Cambridge: W. Heffer & Sons, Ltd., 1933.

————. *Commentary of Theodore of Mopsuestia on the Nicene Creed*. Woodbrooke Studies: Christian Documents in Syriac, Arabic and Garshuni, Edited and Translated with a Critical Apparatus, vol. 5. Cambridge: W. Heffer & Sons, Ltd., 1932.

O'Brien, Thomas, ed. *Documents on the Liturgy, 1968–1979: Conciliar, Papal and Curial Texts*. Washington, D.C.: International Commission on English in the Liturgy, 1982.

Schaff, Philip, ed. *Chrysostom: On the Priesthood, Ascetic Treatises, Select Homilies and Letters, Homilies on the Statutes*. Nicene and Post-Nicene Fathers. First series. Vol. 9. Peabody, Mass.: Hendrickson Pub., Inc., 1995. Originally published by Christian Literature Pub. Co., 1889.

Wilkinson, John. *Egeria's Travels to the Holy Land*. Rev. ed. Newly translated with supporting documents and notes by John Wilkinson. Jerusalem: Ariel Publishing House, 1981.

Secondary Sources

Anderson, E. Byron. "Performance, Practice and Meaning in Christian Baptism." *Worship* 69:6 (November 1995): 482–504.

Anderson, William A. "Period Four—Mystagogy." In *Journeying through the RCIA*. Dubuque: Wm. C. Brown, 1984.

————. "Postbaptismal Catechesis or Mystagogy." In *RCIA: A Total Parish Process*. Dubuque: Brown Publishing, 1989. 102–104.

Baerwald, Jeffrey P. "Mystagogy." In *The New Dictionary of Sacramental Worship*. Edited by Peter E. Fink. Collegeville, Minn.: The Liturgical Press, 1990. 881–883.

————. "Mystagogy: Structure, Content, Task." *Catechumenate* 8:3 (May 1986): 4–15.

Bradshaw, Paul F. "Redating the Apostolic Tradition: Some Preliminary Steps." In *Rule of Prayer, Rule of Faith: Essays in Honor of Aidan Kavanagh, O.S.B.* Edited by Nathan Mitchell and John Baldovin. Collegeville, Minn.: The Liturgical Press, 1996. 3–17.

Burns Senseman, Rita. "Mystagogy: Life after Birth." *Catechumenate* 17:1 (January 1995): 25–30.

Catholic Church. Congregation for Divine Worship. "Preparing and Celebrating the Paschal Feasts." In *Initiation and Its Seasons*. Edited by Virgil C. Funk. Washington, D.C.: The Pastoral Press, 1990. 27–54.

Catholic Church. National Conference of Catholic Bishops. *Christian Initiation of Adults: A Commentary*. Study Text 10. Washington, D.C.: United States Catholic Conference, 1985.

———. *Fulfilled in Your Hearing*. Washington, D.C.: United States Catholic Conference, 1982.

———. *Music in Catholic Worship*. Washington, D.C.: United States Catholic Conference, 1983.

———. *National Statutes for the Catechumenate*. Washington, D.C.: United States Catholic Conference, 1986.

———. "Sacraments of Initiation and Mystagogy." In *Christian Initiation of Adults: A Commentary*. Study Text 10. Washington, D.C.: United States Catholic Conference, 1985. 67–77.

Chriszt, Dennis. "Mystagogy: Celebrating the Mysteries of the Church." *Worship and Ministry* (Office of Liturgy, Diocese of Orlando) 12:4 (Fall 1992): 10–19.

Clader, Linda L. "Preaching the Liturgical Narrative: The Easter Vigil and the Language of Myth." *Worship* 72:2 (March 1998): 147–161.

Cross, F. L., et al., eds. *The Oxford Dictionary of the Christian Church*. 2nd ed. London: Oxford University Press, 1974.

Curtin, Rosalie, et al. *RCIA: A Practical Approach to Christian Initiation*. Dubuque: Wm. C. Brown Co., Publishers, 1981.

Dalton, William. "The First Epistle of Peter." In *The New Jerome Biblical Commentary*. Edited by Raymond Brown et al. Englewood Cliffs, N.J.: Prentice Hall, 1990.

DeGidio, Sandra. "Dying, Rising, and Living: Rituals of Mystagogy." In *RCIA: The Rites Revisited*. Minneapolis: Winston Press, 1984.

Dooley, Catherine. "From the Visible to the Invisible: Mystagogy in the Catechism of the Catholic Church." *The Living Light* (Spring 1995): 19–28.

Driscoll, Michael S. "Symbol, Mystery, and Catechesis: Toward a Mystagogical Approach." *Liturgical Ministry* (Spring 1998): 67–75.

Duggan, Robert D. "Mystagogia and Continuing Conversion: RCIA Success Stories." In *Christian Initiation Resources Reader, Vol. 4: Mystagogia and Ministries*. New York: William H. Sadlier, Inc., 1984.

———. "We Are Bread for One Another." *Christian Initiation* 23 (April/May, 1997): 1–3.

Dujarier, Michel. "The Period of Postbaptismal Catechesis (Mystagogy)." In *The Rites of Christian Initiation: Historical and Pastoral Reflections*. Translated by Kevin Hart. New York: Sadlier, 1979. 93–97.

Dunning, James B. "Church As Initiating Community." Forum Institute Participant Packet. Falls Church, Va.: North American Forum on the Catechumenate, 1995.

———. "Demystifying Mystagogy." *Catechumenate* 17:3 (May 1995): 29–33.

———. *Echoing God's Word: Formation for Catechists and Homilists in a Catechumenal Church*. Arlington, Va: North American Forum on the Catechumenate, 1993.

———. "Let There Be Mystagogy." *Forum Newsletter* 12:2 (Spring 1995): 1, 6, 10.

———. "The Period of Mystagogy." In *New Wine, New Wineskins: Exploring the RCIA*. New York: Sadlier, 1981. 89–100.

———. "The Stages of Initiation: Part IV. The Sacraments of Initiation and Afterwards." In *Becoming a Catholic Christian: A Symposium on Christian Initiation*. Organized and directed by Christiane Brusselmans. Gen. ed. William J. Reedy. New York: Sadlier, 1981.

Faucher, W. Thomas. "Easter Day and Easter Time: Beginning to Make the Fifty Days Come Alive." In *Initiation and Its Seasons*. Edited by Virgil C. Funk. Washington, D.C.: The Pastoral Press, 1990.

Field, Anne. *From Darkness to Light: What It Meant to Become a Christian in the Early Church*. Ann Arbor: Servant Books, 1978.

Fragomeni, Richard. "Wounded in Extraordinary Depths: Towards a Contemporary Mystagogia." In *A Promise of Presence*. Washington, D.C.: The Pastoral Press, 1992. 115–137.

Goodwin, Rick. "Mystagogy: Mission Oriented." *Christian Initiation* 11 (April/May 1995): 4–5.

Gullage, Moya; James T. Morgan; and Gail Schneider, eds. *Christian Initiation Resources Reader, Vol. 4: Mystagogia and Ministries.* New York: Sadlier, 1984.

Gusmer, Charles W. "Celebrating the Easter Season." In *Christian Initiation Resources Reader, Vol. 4: Mystagogia and Ministries.* New York: William H. Sadlier, Inc., 1984.

Harmless, William. *Augustine and the Catechumenate.* Collegeville, Minn.: The Liturgical Press, 1995.

Hixon, Barbara. "Part VI: The Mystagogical Mentality." In *RCIA Spirituality: Formation for the Catechumenate Team.* San Jose: Resource Publications, Inc., 1997.

Johnson, Maxwell E. "Back Home at the Font: Eight Implications of a Baptismal Spirituality." *Worship* 71:6 (November 1997): 482–503.

Joncas, Jan Michael. *Preaching the Rites of Christian Initiation.* Forum Essays. Chicago: Liturgy Training Publications, 1994.

Kavanagh, Aidan. "Period of Postbaptismal Catechesis or Mystagogy." In *The Shape of Baptism: The Rite of Christian Initiation.* Collegeville, Minn.: The Liturgical Press, 1991.

Kazhdan, Alexander P., ed. *The Oxford Dictionary of Byzantium.* Oxford: University Press, 1991.

Kelly, Maureen. "Successful Mystagogia." *Christian Initiation* 23 (April/May 1997): 8.

Kemp, Raymond B. "Mystagogia—Time to Be Fully Alive." *Christian Initiation Resources* 4:1 (1984): 54–69.

———. "The Mystagogical Experience." In *Christian Initiation Resources Reader, Vol. 4: Mystagogia and Ministries.* New York: William H. Sadlier, Inc., 1984.

King, Eugene. "Initiation and Immersion in the Reign of God." *Catechumenate* (May 1998): 2–11.

Klein, Gregory L. "We Have Seen His Glory: Preparing People for Life in a Eucharistic Community." *Catechumenate* 17:2 (March 1995): 22–28.

Krisak, Tony. "Together in the Mystery." *Christian Initiation* 18 (June/July 1996): 4–5.

Lee, James Michael. *The Content of Religious Instruction: A Social Science Approach.* Birmingham, Ala.: Religious Education Press, Inc., 1985.

Lewinski, Ron. *The Guide for Sponsors*. Rev. ed. Chicago: Liturgy Training Publications, 1987.

———. *Welcoming the New Catholic*. 3rd ed. Chicago: Liturgy Training Publications, 1993.

Lidner, Thomas. "Mystagogy, The Mystery of the Fifty Days." *Catechumenate* 17:2 (March 1995): 9–15.

Lopresti, James. "Community Mystagogy." *Catechumenate* 10:3 (May 1987): 27–33.

———. "Transformation of Promise: Operative Meanings of the Rite of Christian Initiation of Adults from the Initiands Perspective." PhD diss., Boston University, 1981.

Lucinio, Jeanette M. "Catechesis Based on Liturgy of the Word." *Liturgical Ministry* (Spring 1998): 83–88.

Matthews, Susan F. "Celebrating New Life in Christ: Mystagogy and the Book of Revelation, Part One." *Catechumenate* (January 1998): 2–19.

———. "Celebrating New Life in Christ: Mystagogy and the Book of Revelation, Part Two." *Catechumenate* (March 1998): 2–23.

Mauck, M. *Shaping a House for the Church*. Chicago: Liturgy Training Publications, 1990.

Mazza, Enrico. *Mystagogy: A Theology of Liturgy in the Patristic Age*. Translated by Matthew J. O'Connell. New York: Pueblo Publishing, 1990.

McMahon, J. Michael. "Fourth Period: Postbaptismal Catechesis or Mystagogy." In *The Rite of Christian Initiation of Adults: A Liturgical Commentary*. Washington, D.C.: Federation of Diocesan Liturgical Commissions, 1986.

Morris, Thomas H. "Mission: Members vs. Disciples." *Christian Initiation* 11 (April/May 1995): 1–3.

———. "Mystagogy: A Continuing Experience." *Christian Initiation* 18 (June/July 1996): 1–3.

———. "Period of Post-Baptism Catechesis or Mystagogy." In *The RCIA: Transforming the Church: A Resource for Pastoral Implementation*. New York: Paulist Press, 1989.

Oakham, Ron. "The Extended Mystagogy: Indictment or Wisdom?" *Catechumenate* 14:3 (May 1992): 17–23.

———. "Sowing for a Good Harvest: The Underpinning of Mystagogy." *Catechumenate* 12:1 (January 1990): 22–27.

O'Brien, John J. "The Results of a Questionnaire on the RCIA." *Liturgy 80* (February/March 1989): 9–11.

Ostdiek, Gilbert. "Liturgy As Catechesis for Life." *Liturgical Ministry* (Spring 1998): 76–82.

Paris, Aline. "Prepare Yourself for the Journey: The Role of the Scrutinies in the Rite of Christian Initiation of Adults." DMin thesis, Catholic Theological Union at Chicago, 1994.

Quasten, Johannes. *Patrology*. The Golden Age of Greek Patristic Literature from the Council of Nicaea to the Council of Chalcedon, vol. 3. Westminster, Md.: Christian Classics, Inc., 1984. Reprint of an earlier edition. Utrecht, Holland: Spectrum, 1950.

Raiche, Diane Dudoit. "Catechists' Corner." *Christian Initiation* 23 (April/May 1997): 5.

———. "Liturgical Catechesis." *Christian Initiation* 23 (April/May 1997): 4.

Regan, David. *Experience the Mystery: Pastoral Possibilities for Christian Mystagogy*. Collegeville, Minn.: The Liturgical Press, 1994.

Riley, Hugh M. *Christian Initiation: A Comparative Study of the Interpretation of the Baptismal Liturgy in the Mystagogical Writings of Cyril of Jerusalem, John Chrystostom, Theodore of Mopsuestia, and Ambrose of Milan*. Washington, D.C.: The Catholic University of America Press, 1974.

Searle, Mark. "Mystagogy: Reflecting on the Easter Experience." *Assembly* 9 (February 1983): 197.

Smith, Pamela. *Life after Easter: Mystagogy Is for Everyone*. Mahwah, N.J.: Paulist Press, 1993.

Steffen, Donna. "Forming Disciples: Mystagogic Catechesis." *Christian Initiation* 23 (April/May 1997): 6–7.

Upton, Julia. "The Honeymoon." In *Journey into Mystery: A Companion to the RCIA*. New York: Paulist Press, 1986.

Weind, Teresita. "Mystagogue." In *A Catechumenate Needs Everybody: Study Guides for Parish Ministers*. Chicago: Liturgy Training Publications, 1988. 57–58.

———. "Mystagogy: Where Mystery Meets Ministry." *Catechumenate* 9:3 (May 1987): 20–24.

Weiss, Joseph E. "Liturgy and Catechesis." *Liturgical Ministry* (Spring 1998): 57–66.

Yarnold, Edward. *The Awe-Inspiring Rites of Initiation: The Origins of the RCIA.* 2nd ed. Collegeville, Minn.: The Liturgical Press, 1994.

Resources for Mystagogy

Baumbach, Gerard F. *Experiencing Mystagogy: The Sacred Pause of Easter.* New York: Paulist Press, 1996.

Boyer, Mark G. *Mystagogy: Liturgical Paschal Spirituality for Lent and Easter.* New York: Alba House, 1990.

Bruns, William R. *Cenacle Sessions: A Modern Mystagogy.* New York: Paulist Press, 1991.

————. *Easter Bread: Reflections on the Gospels of the Easter Season for Neophytes and Their Companions.* New York: Paulist Press, 1991.

Chilson, Richard. *A Lenten Pilgrimage—Dying and Rising in the Lord: A Manual for Ministry in the Lenten Catechumenate.* New York: Paulist Press, 1983.

Ellebracht, Mary Pierre. *The Easter Passage: The RCIA Experience.* Minneapolis: Winston Press, 1983.

Hinman Powell, Karen, and Joseph P. Sinwell, eds. *Ninety Days: Resources for Lent and Eastertime in the RCIA.* New York: Paulist Press, 1989.

Maxwell, Bernard J.; Judy Foster; and Jill Shirvington. *Easter for Fifty Days.* Mystic, Conn.: Twenty-Third Publications, 1989.

Ramshaw, Gail, ed. *Words Around the Fire: Reflections on the Scriptures of the Easter Vigil.* Chicago: Liturgy Training Publications, 1990.

————. *Words Around the Font.* Chicago: Liturgy Training Publications, 1994.

————. *Words Around the Table.* Chicago: Liturgy Training Publications, 1991.

Sinwell, Joseph P., ed. *Come Follow Me: Resources for the Period of Inquiry in the RCIA.* New York: Paulist Press, 1990.

Literature on Methods

Anderson, E. Byron. "Performance, Practice and Meaning in Christian Baptism." *Worship* 69:6 (November 1995): 482–504.

Bailey, Raymond, contributing ed. "A Theological Model." In *Hermeneutics for Preaching: Approaches to Contemporary Interpretation of Scripture*. Nashville: Broadman Press, 1992.

Browning, Don S. *A Fundamental Practical Theology: Descriptive and Strategic Proposals*. Minneapolis: Fortress Press, 1991.

Carey, Raymond P. "Realizing the Vision: How Does the Diocesan Vocation Office Help Identify and Assess the Candidate." Paper presented at Behavioral Assessment of Candidates for Priesthood and Religious Life workshop sponsored by the National Religious Vocations Conference, Bloomington, Minn., April 22–24, 1994.

———. "Theological and Psychological Perspectives: Theoretical Underpinnings." Paper presented at Behavioral Assessment of Candidates for Priesthood and Religious Life workshop sponsored by the National Religious Vocations Conference, Bloomington, Minn., April 22–24, 1994.

Gremillion, Joseph, and Jim Castelli. *The Emerging Parish: The Notre Dame Study of Catholic Life Since Vatican II*. San Francisco: Harper & Row, 1987.

Groome, Thomas H. *Sharing Faith: A Comprehensive Approach to Religious Education and Pastoral Ministry*. San Francisco: Harper Collins, 1991.

Hoffman, Lawrence A. *Beyond the Text: A Holistic Approach to Liturgy*. Bloomington: Indiana University Press, 1987.

Irwin, Kevin W. *Context and Text: Method in Liturgical Theology*. Collegeville, Minn.: The Liturgical Press, 1994.

Kelleher, Margaret Mary. "Liturgical Theology: A Task and A Method." *Worship* 62 (1988): 2–25.

McBride, Alfred. *A Catholic Learning Guide for Adult Initiation: The Search for God, Self, and Church*. Washington, D.C.: Paulist National Catholic Evangelization Association, 1984.

[Mitchell, Nathan.] "Semiotics." *Liturgy Digest* 2:1 (Fall 1994): 66–78.

———. "Semiotics of the Visual Arts." *Liturgy Digest* 2:1 (Fall 1994): 78–89.

Nygren, David J., and Miriam D. Ukeritis. *The Future of Religious Orders in the United States: Transformation and Commitment.* Westport, Conn.: Praeger, 1993.

Ostdiek, Gilbert. "Ritual and Transformation: Reflections on Liturgy and the Social Sciences." *Liturgical Ministry* 2 (Spring 1993): 38–48.

Poling, James, and Donald Miller. *Foundations for a Practical Theology of Ministry.* Nashville: Abingdon Press, 1985.

Schreiter, Robert J. *Constructing Local Theologies.* Maryknoll, N.Y.: Orbis Books, 1993.

————. *The New Catholicity: Theology Between the Global and the Local.* Maryknoll, N.Y.: Orbis Books, 1997.

————. "Precious Blood Spirituality and CPPS Identity." *CPPS Newsletter* 221 (August 1985).

Senn, Frank C. "'Worship Alive': An Analysis and Critique of 'Alternate Worship Services.'" *Worship* 69 (May 1995): 194–224.

Tracy, David. "Interpretation of the Bible and Interpretation Theory." In *A Short History of the Interpretation of the Bible.* 2nd ed. Edited by Robert M. Grant. Minneapolis: Fortress Press, 1984.

Warren, Michael. "Speaking and Learning in the Local Church: A Look at the Material Conditions." *Worship* 69 (January 1995): 28–50.

Whitehead, James D., and Evelyn Eaton Whitehead. *Method in Ministry: Theological Reflection and Christian Ministry.* New York: Seabury Press, 1980.